GW01032860

C O
KINS
STREET
ATLAS
&
GUIDE

CONTENTS

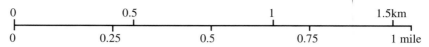

Scale of maps is 1:15,000 (4.2 inches to 1 mile)

0	0.5	1	1.5km
0	0.25	0.5	0.75	1 mile

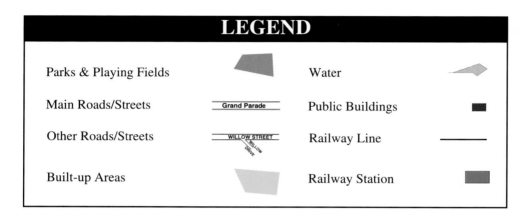

LEGEND

Parks & Playing Fields

Water

Main Roads/Streets — Grand Parade

Public Buildings

Other Roads/Streets — WILLOW STREET / WILLOW DRIVE

Railway Line

Built-up Areas

Railway Station

© Causeway Press (N.I.) July 2000

The maps on pages 4 to 21 are based upon Ordnance Survey Ireland by permission of the Government (Permit No. 7084).

Printed by The Universities Press (Belfast) Ltd.

Edited by Paul Slevin. Comments, suggestions and inquiries should be addressed to him at the address below. Published by Causeway Press (N.I.), Enterprise House, Balloo Avenue, Bangor, N.Ireland BT19 7QT. Phone (028) 91271525. Fax (028) 91270080.
E-mail paulslevin@talk21.com

DISTRIBUTION: Distributed by News Brothers Ltd (phone Cork 4964355), Eason Wholesale Books Ltd (phone Dublin 862 2111), Argosy Libraries Ltd (phone Dublin 855 2727). Quote ISBN 1 872600 58 1.

ACKNOWLEDGEMENTS: Special thanks go the research team of Catherine Coyle, Ashley Adsett and Paul Adsett. Additional thanks go to Cork Corporation, Cork Kerry Tourism and to Denis Burke at Bus Eireann.

CORK
KINSALE
STREET
ATLAS
&
GUIDE

We all like to kill two birds with one stone, so to speak, but the Cork & Kinsale Street Atlas & Guide is that extremely rare bird which offers several different products for the price of one.

Firstly, it is a street atlas of the greater Cork area, based on the latest Ordnance Survey. These maps, together with separate road and city centre maps, will help you to navigate your way through and around the city.

Secondly, it is a detailed guide to the best of what Cork and Kinsale have to offer. Whether you are visiting for the first time or have lived here all your life, our aim is to help you make the most of this vibrant and colourful part of Ireland.

The guide is written and published in Ireland, and is based on contributions from people who have immersed themselves in the Cork social scene with scant regard to their need of sleep and the health of their livers. Having said that, we are always keen to hear alternative views. If you have any recommendations to make, or any contrary views to express regarding any of our choices, please write, fax or e-mail to the addresses given on the page opposite. Any contributions which we use in the future will be acknowledged and a copy of the next edition will be sent in return for the best letters.

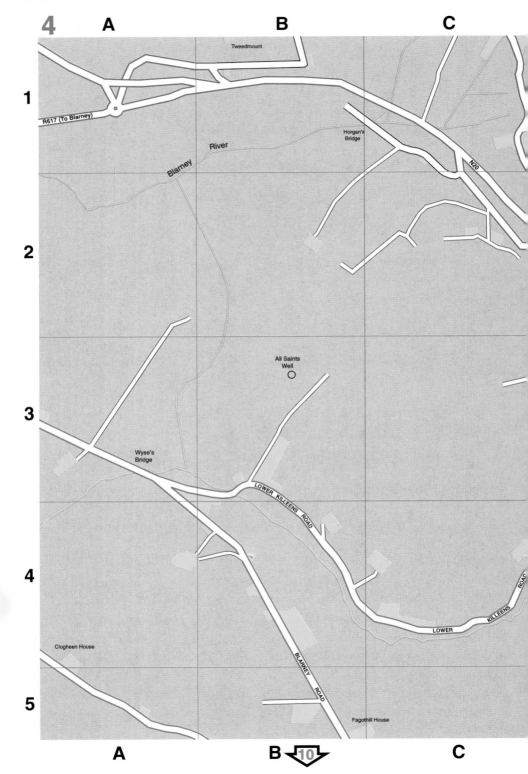

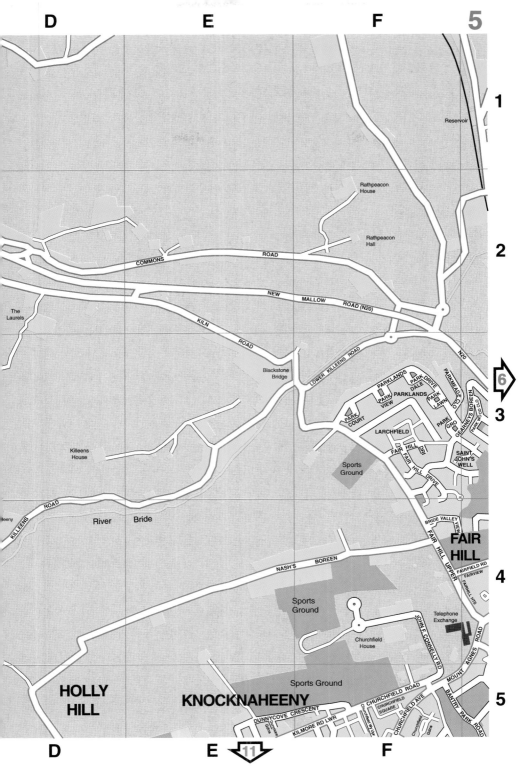

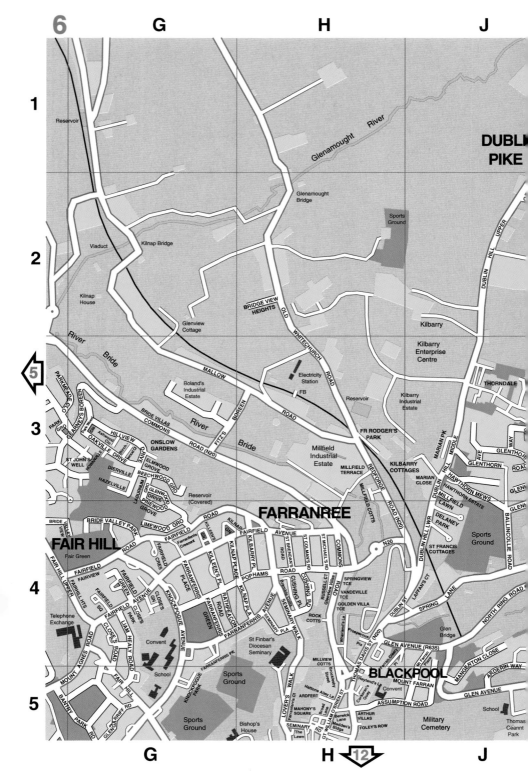

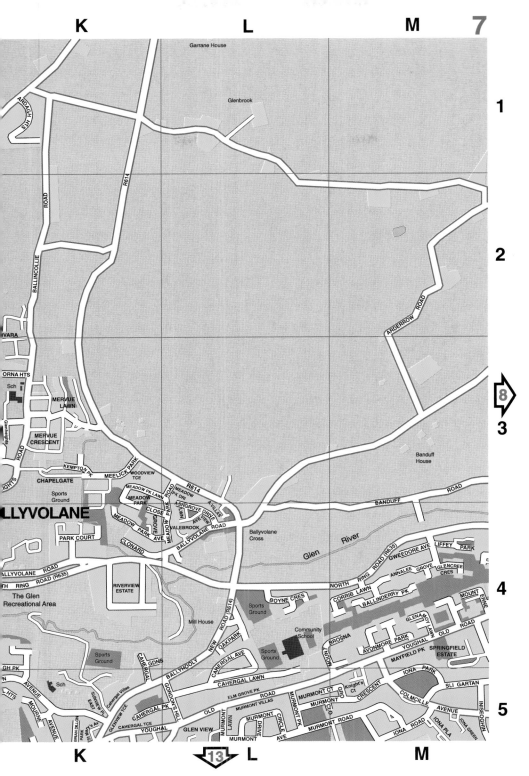

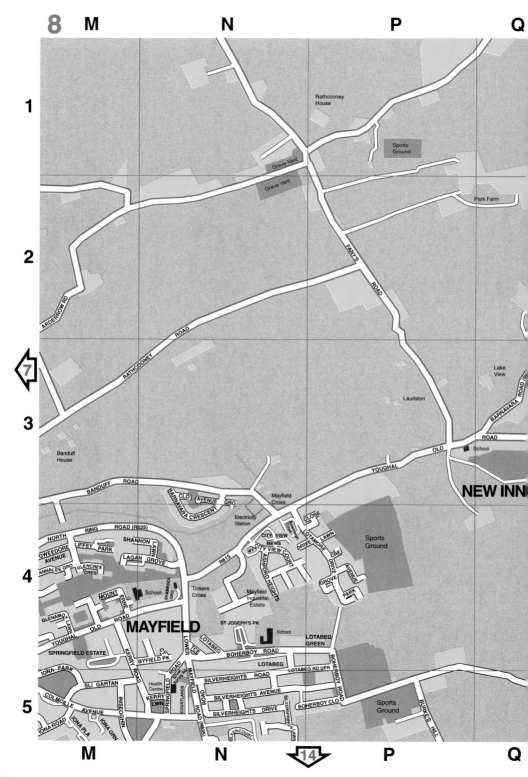

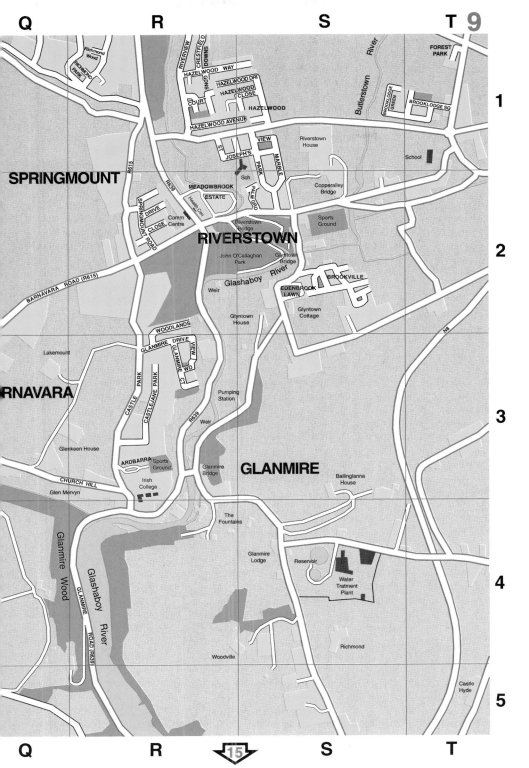

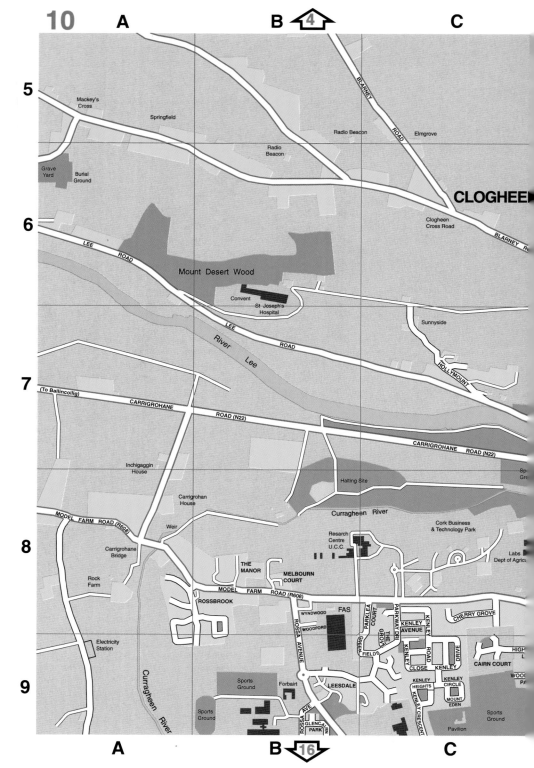

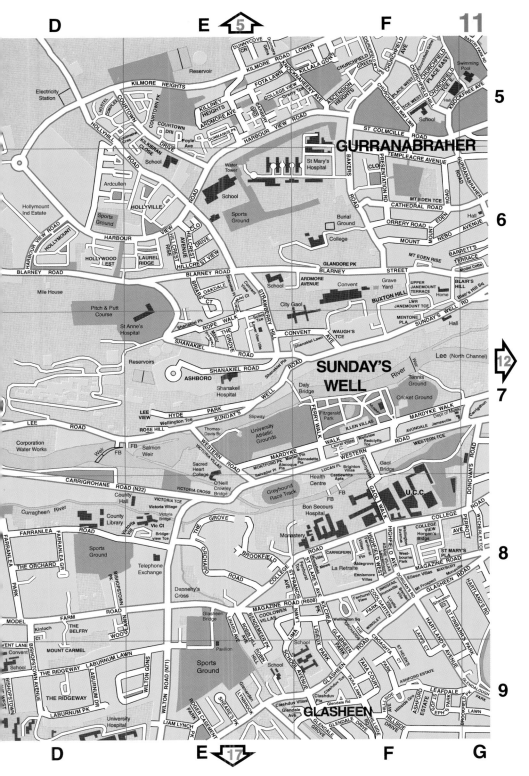

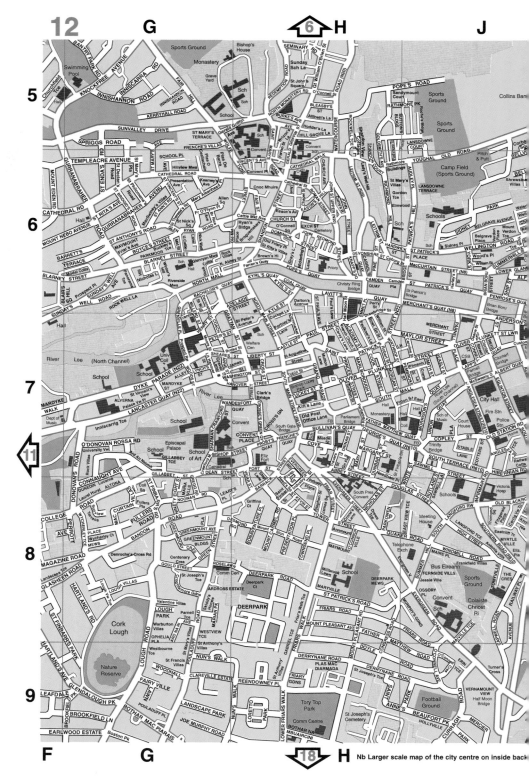

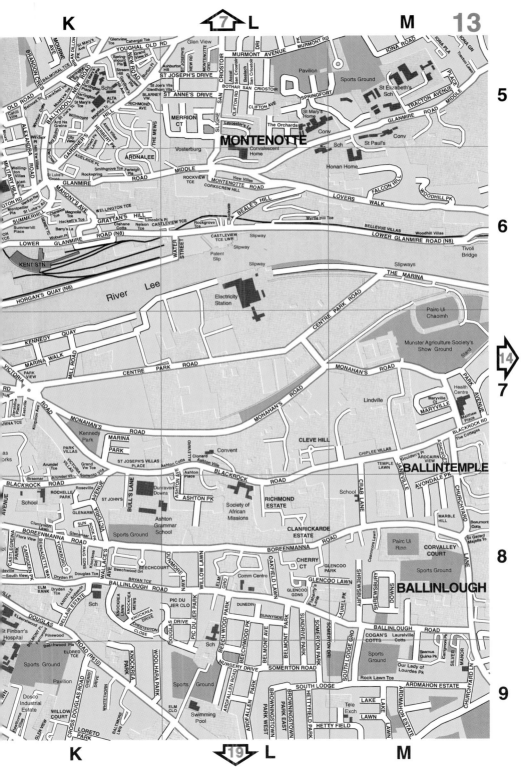

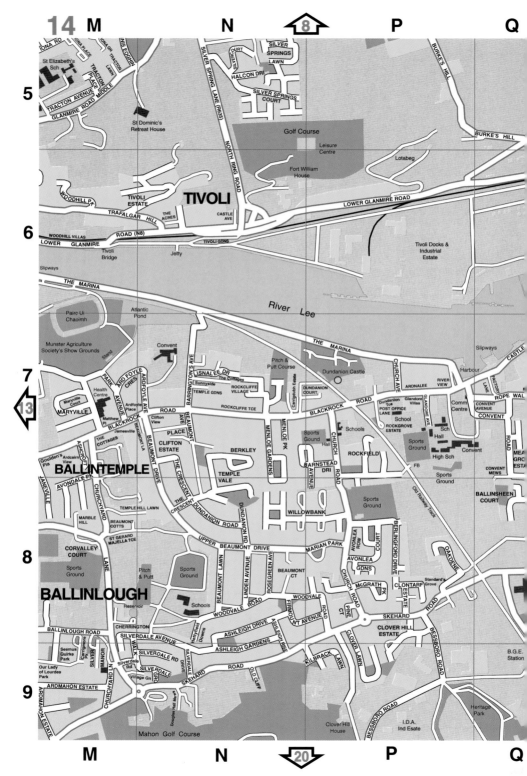

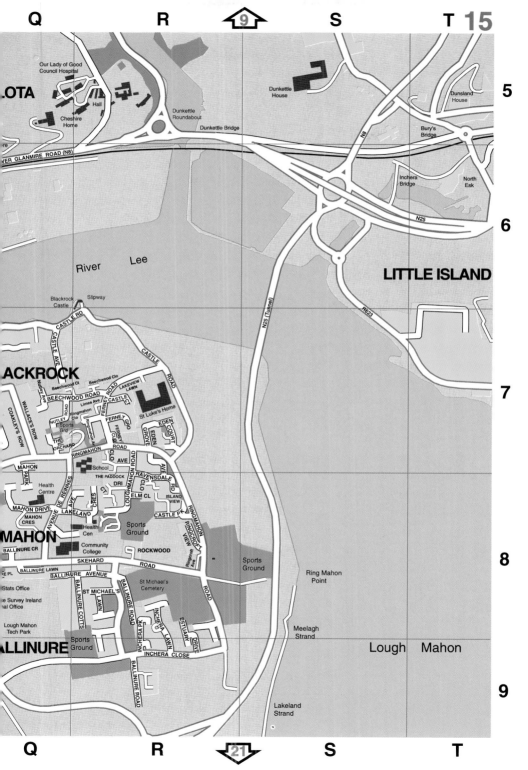

Q R S T

Our Lady of Good
Council Hospital

LOTA

Hall

Cheshire
Home

Dunkettle
House

Dunsland
House

5

Dunkettle
Roundabout

Dunkettle Bridge

Bury's
Bridge

ER GLANMIRE ROAD (N8)

N8

Inchera
Bridge

North
Esk

6

N25

River Lee

LITTLE ISLAND

Blackrock
Castle

Slipway

CASTLE RD

CASTLE AVE

CASTLE ROAD

N25 (Tunnel)

R623

ACKROCK

7

Beechwood Ct

Beechwood Clo

BEECHWOOD ROAD

CASTLE ROAD

FERNEY ROAD

LAKEVIEW
LAWN

Nutley Ave

Limes Ave

CASTLE

St Luke's Home

WALLACE'S ROW

Ringmahon

Ringmahon Av

FERNEY

EDEN COURT

EDEN GROVE

COAKLEY'S ROW

NUTLEY
Clo

THE
ORCHARD

Sports
Grd

FERNEY
ROAD

RINGMAHON ROAD

CLO
AVE

School

MAHON
PARK

Health
Centre

THE PADDOCK

DRI

RAVENSDALE

LOUGHMAHON ROAD

AVE
RD

MAHON DRIVE

AVENUE DE RENNES

CRES

ELM CL

ISLAND
VIEW

RINGMAHON ROAD

RINGCROFT

Ringmahon Ave

VIEW

MAHON
CRES

LAKELAND

CASTLE PK

MAHON

Health
Cen

Sports
Ground

BALLINURE CR

Community
College

ROCKWOOD

8

SKEHARD
ROAD

Sports
Ground

Ring Mahon
Point

E PL

BALLINURE LAWN

BALLINURE AVENUE

Stats Office

BALLINURE COTTS

BALLINURE ROAD

ST MICHAEL'S
LAWN

St Michael's
Cemetery

BALLINURE ROAD

INCHERA PK

INCHERA LAWN

ESTUARY DRIVE

INCHERA CLOSE

Meelagh
Strand

Lough Mahon

e Survey Ireland
nal Office

Lough Mahon
Tech Park

Sports
Ground

ALLINURE

9

Lakeland
Strand

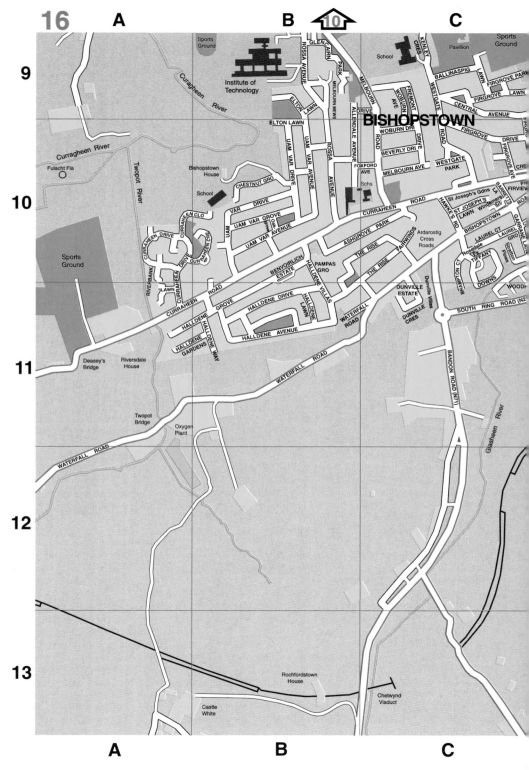

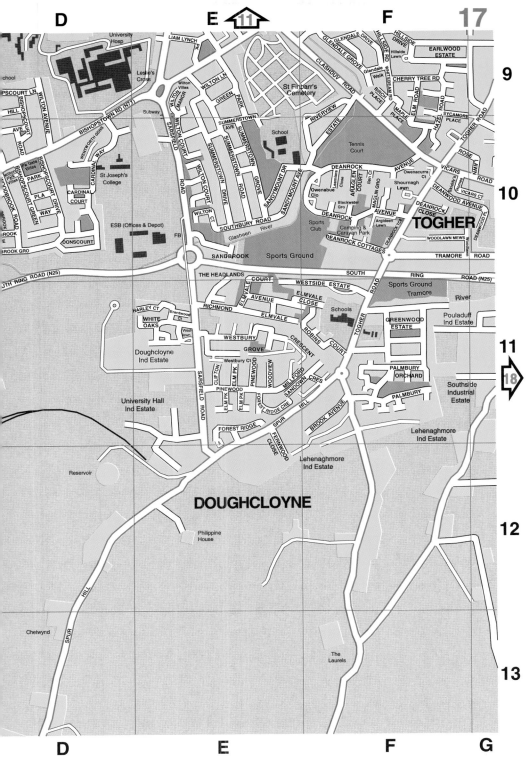

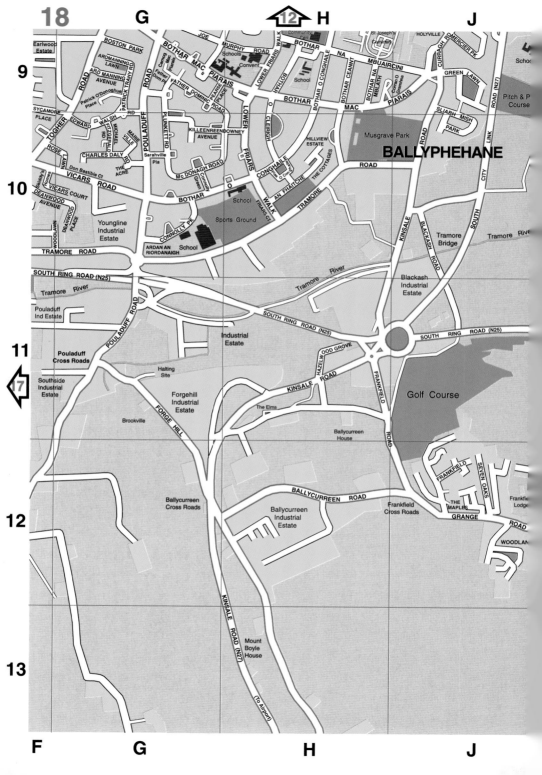

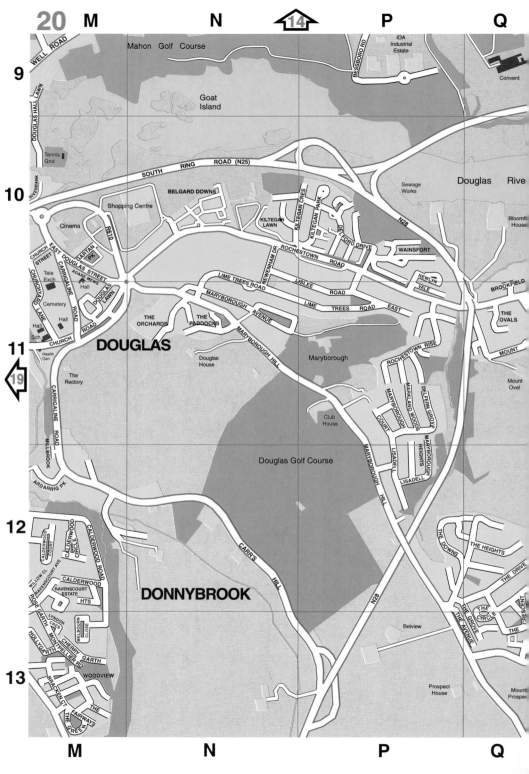

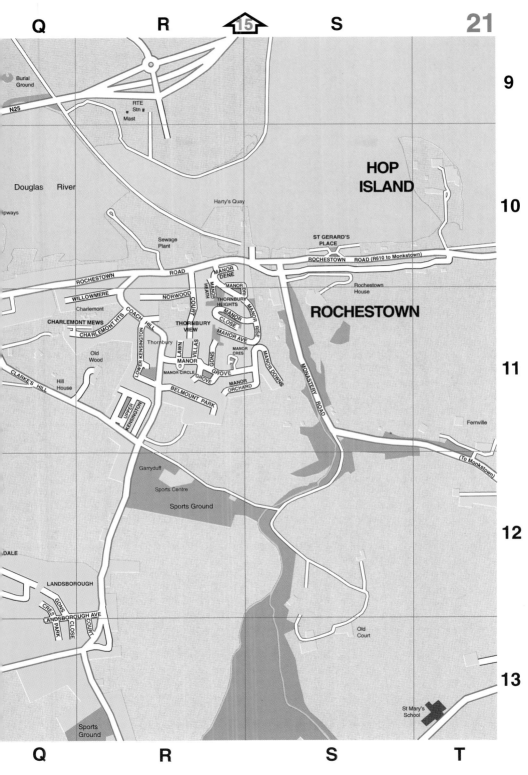

9

Burial
Ground

N25

Douglas   River

10

lipways

Harty's Quay

HOP
ISLAND

Sewage
Plant

ST GERARD'S
PLACE

ROCHESTOWN   ROAD (R610 to Monkstown)

ROCHESTOWN   ROAD

Rochestown
House

WILLOWMERE

NORWOOD

MANOR
DENE

MANOR

MANOR
HEATH

THORNBURY
HEIGHTS

MANOR DRI

MANOR RISE

ROCHESTOWN

Charlemont

CHARLEMONT MEWS

CHARLEMONT HTS

COACH   HILL

THORNBURY
VIEW

MANOR
CLOSE

MANOR AVE

LOWER KENSINGTON

Thornbury

COURT

LAWN

VILLAS

SNDS   GROVE

MANOR
CRES

MANOR
DOWNS

Old
Wood

MANOR

MANOR CIRCLE   GROVE

MANOR
ORCHARD

11

CLARKE'S   HILL

Hill
House

UPPER
KENSINGTON

BELMOUNT PARK

MONASTERY   ROAD

Fernville

(To Monkstown)

Garryduff

Sports Centre

Sports Ground

12

DALE

LANDSBOROUGH

GDNS

CRES

CLOSE

COURT

LANDSBOROUGH AVE

PARK

Old
Court

13

St Mary's
School

Sports
Ground

KINSALE

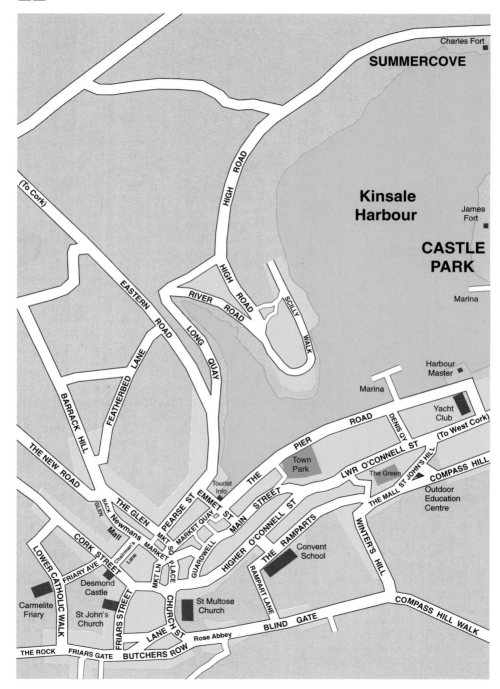

0   50m

Charles Fort

SUMMERCOVE

(To Cork)

HIGH ROAD

Kinsale Harbour

James Fort

CASTLE PARK

Marina

HIGH ROAD

RIVER ROAD

SCILLY WALK

EASTERN ROAD

LONG QUAY

FEATHERBED LANE

BARRACK HILL

Harbour Master

Marina

THE NEW ROAD

PIER ROAD

DENIS QY

Yacht Club

(To West Cork)

COMPASS HILL

THE GLEN

BACK GLEN

Newmans Mall

Town Park

THE MALL

ST JOHN'S HILL

The Green

LWR O'CONNELL ST

Tourist Info

PEARSE ST

EMMET ST

THE STREET

MAIN STREET

Outdoor Education Centre

CORK STREET

MKT SQ

MARKET

GUARDWELL

HIGHER O'CONNELL ST

THE RAMPARTS

WINTER'S HILL

FRIARY AVE

Chairman's Lane

MKT LN

PLACE

MARKET QUAY

Convent School

LOWER CATHOLIC WALK

Desmond Castle

St John's Church

FRIARS STREET

CHURCH ST

St Multose Church

RAMPART LANE

COMPASS HILL WALK

Carmelite Friary

LANE

Rose Abbey

BLIND GATE

THE ROCK

FRIARS GATE

BUTCHERS ROW

STREET INDEX

Due to insufficient space, some streets and/or their names have been omitted from the street map. Street names below which are prefixed by a * are not represented on the map, but they can be located by referring in the index to the name of the street which follows in brackets. Kinsale streets are in blue.

23

STREET INDEX

STREET INDEX

STREET INDEX

STREET INDEX

STREET INDEX

Cork, which gets its name from the Gaelic, *Corcaigh*, meaning 'a marshy place', is Ireland's third largest city with a population of around 175,000. The River Lee runs through the centre of the city, splitting into two different channels in the western suburbs and rejoining at the Custom House in the east. The city centre thereby sits on an island, linked by a series of bridges. As you might imagine, this can be confusing if you are driving in Cork for the first time, as much of the traffic is shunted around a one way system which necessitates the crossing and recrossing of the river.

Cork City Hall reflected in the waters of the River Lee

Cork received its first charter in 1185 but its early development dates back to the 7th century when St Fin Barre founded a monastic settlement in 606 near to the site where the current St Fin Barre's Cathedral stands. The Vikings were regular visitors during the 9th, 10th and 11th centuries, and the city was destroyed by fire several times during this period.

In 1172 the local chieftain, Dermot McCarthy, Prince of Desmond and King of Cork, surrendered the city to the the Anglo Normans who had been sent by King Henry II, and an English governor and garrison were installed for the first time.

Prince John granted the town its first charter in 1185 and 1199 marks the date of the first recorded Mayor of Cork, John Dispenser. Although English laws were nominally in force from this time, Cork's citizens retained their independent nature and the city was effectively ruled by its wealthy merchants.

Perkin Warbeck, pretender to the English throne, came to Cork in 1492 and was supported by Cork's Mayor, John Waters. Both returned to England where Warbeck proclaimed himself Richard IV, King of England and Lord of Ireland. Waters was later tried in London for high treason and hanged with Warbeck at Tyburn in 1499.

By 1542 Henry VIII had proclaimed himself King of Ireland as well as England, and the Reformation came to Ireland. Monasteries in and around Cork were dissolved, and their land and possessions were distributed to families loyal to the crown.

With Charles I beheaded and the English monarchy abolished, Oliver Cromwell landed in Ireland with a large army in 1649, ushering in a particularly bloody and savage era in Irish history. The monarchy was restored in 1660 and by 1685 the Catholic King James II was on the throne and Ireland was soon to become a battlefield for a religious war involving most of Europe's major powers. King James landed at Kinsale in 1688 and frequently stayed in Cork at the Dominican Friary on Crosse's Green. Forces of the Protestant William of Orange laid siege to Cork in 1690 due to the city's support for James. The city surrendered and James later lost the Battle of the Boyne to William who went on to become king. Catholics subsequently suffered under the Penal Laws, Gaelic culture was driven underground, and the seeds were sewn for the struggle for Irish autonomy from England.

Following its surrender, Cork's city walls were allowed to crumble into ruins and the city grew rapidly as a merchant port specialising in the export of butter, beef, grain, textiles, whiskey and porter. Canals were built to bring boats further into the city and the remains of these can be seen on Grand Parade where the mooring posts still stand by the kerbside of what was once a waterway. In the early 18th century, the city received many of the Huguenots who fled from religious persecution in France. Their presence is recalled in the name of French Church Street. Many of the city's fine Georgian buildings were built during this time.

The Act of Union of 1800 brought Ireland into a United Kingdom with Britain, and the seat of political power moved from Dublin to Westminster. A century of political turmoil followed. The potato famine decimated much of Ireland in the late 1840's. Out of a population of 8.5 million, approximately one million starved to death and a further 1.5 million emigrated, mainly to Britain and North America, most of them setting sail from Cobh. The history of the town and its links to shipping and emigration are explored in an interesting exhibition called The Queenstown Story which is housed in Cobh's restored Victorian railway station (see page 41). The famine years served to heighten anti-British sentiment, and an abortive rebellion by the Irish Republican Brotherhood in 1868 led to calls for Irish home rule.

The case for Irish autonomy was taken up in the English parliament at

View of Cork from UCC

Westminster by the Protestant leader Charles Stewart Parnell. Parnell died in 1891, however, leaving a political vacuum which was eventually filled by two cultural movements, the Gaelic League which was set up to revive the Irish Language, and the Irish Literary Renaissance. This cultural nationalism developed into political nationalism with the establishment of Sinn Féin (Ourselves Alone), a political movement which advocated a boycott of the English Parliament. With Britain engaged in the First World War, Sinn Féin organised the occupation of several strategic buildings around Dublin, and declared an Irish republic from its headquarters in the General Post Office on Easter Monday 1916.

Cork was closely linked to the republican cause and some of its streets are named after famous Irish republicans. MacCurtain Street is named after a former mayor of the city, Thomas MacCurtain, who was killed in 1920 by the notorious Black & Tans - the nick-name given to demobilised British soldiers drafted in to act as police. His successor as mayor was another republican, Terence McSwiney, who died later the same year in London's Brixton Prison, after spending 74 days on hunger strike.

The 1916 Easter Rising was quashed after six days of fighting with British forces, who numbered 20,000 troops, and 15 of the rebel leaders were later executed. A wave of public sympathy resulted, and Sinn Féin secured an overwhelming victory in the 1918 elections. A War of Independence between British and Irish republican armies soon followed and, after two years of fighting, the Cork general, Michael Collins, signed a treaty in 1921 which resulted in the creation of the Irish Free State, comprising 26 of Ireland's 32 counties. The other six counties became known as Northern Ireland and remained within the United Kingdom.

The 1921 treaty caused division between different factions within Sinn Féin and a bitter Civil War broke out which lasted for a year and saw much bloodshed and destruction in both Dublin and Cork. On signing the treaty, Collins had commented that he was signing his own death warrant, and he was proved right the following year when he was assassinated by anti-treaty forces on the road between Macroom and Bandon. Eamon de Valera won the battle for political control of the new state, and a period of political and cultural conservatism ensued which lasted until the late 1950's.

Ireland was declared a republic in 1949, but it was not until the 1960's that the country started to look outwards. De Valera stepped down in 1959 to assume the figurehead role of Irish President, and a new Taoiseach (Prime Minister), Sean Lemass, assumed power and began a process of modernisation and industrialisation. Perhaps the most defining moment in the recent history of Cork and the rest of the country, however, was Ireland's admission to the European Economic Community in 1973.

Over the past thirty years, Ireland has been transformed from a predominantly agricultural country into a vibrant industrial economy, in which church and government are becoming increasingly disentangled as evidenced by the 1995 referendum result in favour of divorce, and liberalisation of laws in relation to homosexuality and abortion. Cork is fast becoming a modern European city which boasts a young and well educated population that has proved attractive to many foreign investors.

Ireland is now the second biggest exporter of computer software after the US, supplying around 40% of the European market, and Cork plays an important role in this success story with companies such as Apple and Siemens locating in and around the city. Cork is also an important centre for the pharmaceuticals industry with household names such as Smithkline Beecham, Pfizer and Eli Lilly employing more than 3,000 people in the region. Economic progress over the past ten years has been startling, and Ireland's 'Celtic tiger' now produces a per capita income which exceeds that of the UK for the first time in Irish history.

Cork continues to invest in its infrastructure. A £120m drainage scheme will clean up the city's waterways and further enhance the urban environment. Major road improvements have been carried out, including the £100m Jack Lynch Tunnel under the Lee Estuary, and these schemes are helping to ease traffic congestion and attract new investment. A £7m make-over of St Patrick's Street and Grand Parade will help to make the city centre more pedestrian friendly.

Cork is managing to shake off its reputation as a provincial backwater when compared to its more cosmopolitan cousin, Dublin. Although it remains a convenient base from which to explore the beautiful countryside which surrounds it, visitors are coming to the city in increasing numbers to avail of the warm welcome and busy nightlife which are its hallmarks.

Whether you are living here or merely passing through, the sections which follow will try to help you make the best of all that Cork has to offer.

AIR TRAVEL

Cork airport lies about 5 miles south of the city centre and is the gateway for flights to many destinations across Ireland, the UK and Europe. Aer Lingus is Ireland's national airline, operating several domestic services out of Cork in addition to its international routes which leave from Dublin. Other airlines using the airport include Ryanair, British Airways and KLM who meet the travel requirements of the one million passengers who use the facility annually.

Aer Rianta, the airport managers, provide a comprehensive flight information service. Phone (021) 4327100 or access the airport web site on www.aerrianta.ie

International and domestic arrivals and departures share the same terminal building and facilities include a bank, cash machine, information desk, shop, car hire desks and a cafe.

An express coach service operates from outside the main terminal building into the city centre, stopping at the central bus station in Parnell Place. Buses depart every 45 minutes and the single fare is £2.50. Tickets can be bought from the driver and the journey normally takes about 15 minutes, depending on traffic. A cab from the taxi rank in front of the terminal building will take you into the city centre for around £6.

Avis, Budget, Hertz, National and Murrays Europcar all have car hire desks at the airport. Renting a car can be an expensive exercise in Ireland, mainly due to the high cost of insurance, and it usually pays to shop around. Pre-booking through a travel agent will avoid the disappointment of not being able to get hold of a car, which can sometimes happen during the summer months.

FERRY SERVICES

Ferries to Cork arrive at the small town of Ringaskiddy which is a few miles outside the city. Crossing with Swansea Cork Ferries takes about 10 hours but saves a 150 mile drive from Dublin to Cork. Services to France operate during the tourist season with Irish Ferries sailing to Le Havre and Roscoff and Brittany Ferries going to Roscoff and St Malo. On arrival, passengers can catch a bus from the terminal building which will take them the 11 miles into the centre of Cork.

TRAINS

Irish rail services are operated by Iarnród Eireann (Irish Rail) but the only local service covers the 15 miles from Cork to Cobh via Littleisland, Glounthuane, Fota, Carrigaloe, and Rushbrooke. Trains leave hourly throughout the day from Kent Station on Lower Glanmire Road and the journey time to Cobh is 25 minutes.

There are frequent inter city services between Cork and Dublin and between Cork and Tralee. The journey to Dublin takes around three hours and stops en route include Limerick. Stops on the way to Tralee include Millstreet and Killarney and the journey time is about two and a half hours.

Fares & Tickets

Travelling by train tends to cost more than going by bus but there are discounts available for students with an ISIC card (International Student Identity Card), and for anybody under the age of 26 with a European Youth Card. To take advantage of the discounts, however, it is necessary to buy a Travelsave Stamp.

A selection of rail and/or bus passes is available if you intend exploring the country as a whole. For example, £67 will buy you an Irish Explorer rail pass which allows 5 days of travel within any 15 day period on all trains within the Republic of Ireland.

Train Information

Phone Kent Station Inquiries on (021) 4504888.

BUS SERVICES

Bus Eireann (Irish Bus) operates a comprehensive bus service in Cork City as well as a network of services which connect Cork with the rest of Ireland.

City Services

Cork City Bus Services operate from 7am to 11.15pm Monday to Saturday, and from 10am to 11.15pm on Sundays. Most services connect with the city centre. The times shown on bus poles/shelters are the departure times from the terminus.

City fares are charged at a flat rate of 75p per adult and 50p per child. £4 buys unlimited daily travel on all Cork city services for one or two adults and up to three children under 16. An adult weekly ticket is available for £9 and £34 will buy you unlimited travel on all city services for a calendar month.

Suburban Services

Bus Eireann operates a comprehensive service between Cork City and the suburbs. Locations such as Blarney, Kinsale, Ballincollig and Carrigaline are well served with all the major towns also getting a good service. An adult day return to Blarney costs £3.

Airport Bus

A frequent service operates between the airport and the central bus station on Parnell Place. Adult fares are £2.50 single and £3.60 return. A family ticket is available for £7.20. Journey time is approximately 15 minutes.

Long Distance Services

'Expressway' is the name for Bus Eireann's long distance network of services which connect Cork with the rest of Ireland. Frequent services operate between Cork and all major locations such as Dublin, Killarney, Waterford, Limerick, Galway and Kilkenny.

Rambler and Rover Tickets

A range of flexible tickets, ideal for holidaymakers, offers unlimited bus travel for 3, 8 or 15 days. The Rambler ticket covers travel on all Bus Eireann services within the Republic of Ireland while the Rover ticket covers services throughout the whole of Ireland, except for Bus Eireann tours. For example, a three day Rambler ticket allows 3 days travel out of 8 consecutive days and costs £30. An 8 day Rover ticket allows 8 days of travel out of 15 consecutive days and costs £90.

Scenic Day Tours

Bus Eireann operates scenic day tours out of Cork City from May to September. West Cork, Kerry and Clare are the most popular destinations. All tours depart from Parnell Place Bus Station but some tours may be joined at

Blarney and Macroom.

Fares vary from £16 to £20 and concession fares are available for families and children. Pre booking is advisable.

Bus Information

Information on all bus services is available from Bus Eireann Travel Centre, Parnell Place Bus Station. Phone (021) 4508188

Late Night Buses

Bus Eireann operates a late night bus service at the weekends. Buses depart from outside Roches Stores on St Patrick's Street at 12.30am, 1.30am and 2.30am every Friday and Saturday night. There are four routes which are shown in the diagram above. Passengers may alight anywhere en route. Fares are £2 to the city boundary and £3 beyond. For further information contact (021) 4508188.

CAR HIRE

Renting a car in Ireland is usually an expensive exercise but, if you want to explore the country beyond Cork City, a car is a necessity as the public transport system has some severe limitations. Cost will typically be somewhere between £200 and £300 pounds per week depending on the car, the size of the hire company, and the

time of year. Despite the cost, availability can sometimes be a problem during the summer months so it is advisable to book in advance. Listed below are some of the main car hire companies :

Great Island Car Rental `12 J6`
47 MacCurtain St - (021) 4503536

Murrays Europcar
Cork Airport - Ph (021) 4917300

National
Cork Airport - Ph (021) 4320755

BIKE HIRE

Cork city is easily explored on foot but, if you want to get beyond the city, bike hire can be an attractive option, although a good lock and a brave heart in traffic are both important. Hiring a bike typically costs around £8 per day, or £35 per week.

Irish Cycle Hire `13 K6`
Cork Train Station
Phone (021) 4551430

Mylie Murphy `22`
14 Pearse Street, Kinsale
Phone (021) 4772703

Rothar Cycle Tours `12 G8`
2 Bandon Road, Cork
Phone (021) 4313133

WALKING

Many of Cork's attractions are centrally located and easily reached by foot. The Places of Interest section on pages 40-46 details some of the city's landmarks. Guided walking tours can be booked through Cork Tourist Office on Grand Parade where you can also obtain information on a signposted walking tour and the accompanying booklet.

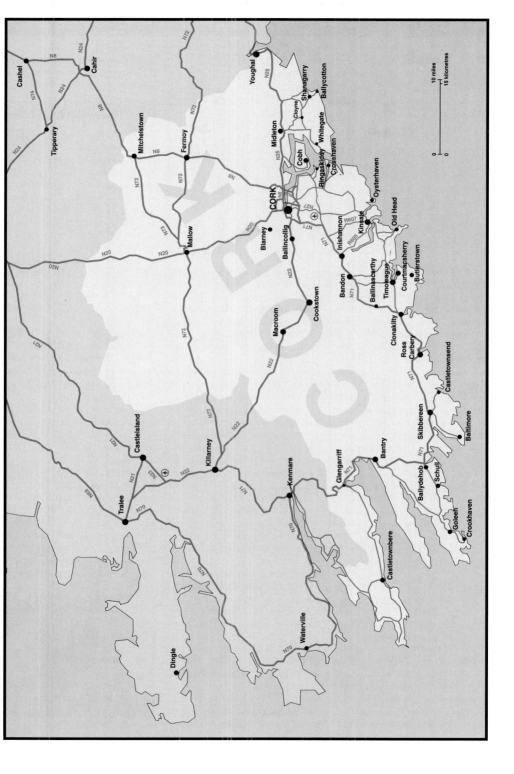

Accommodation Prices

Expensive: Expect to pay in the region of £50 to £80 per night per person sharing, including breakfast. Cheaper rates are usually available at weekends.

Moderate: Expect to pay between £30 and £50 per night per person sharing, including breakfast. Once again, cheaper rates are normally available at weekends.

Budget: Most budget accommodation costs between £15 and £30 per night per person sharing.

Accommodation can be booked directly or through Cork City Tourist Office. Phone (021) 4273251.

As Cork develops, both as a commercial centre and as a tourist destination, new hotels are opening on an annual basis to meet the rising demand for accommodation. Availability can nevertheless be a problem, especially during the summer months, and it is therefore advisable to book your accommodation before you travel. If you have acted on impulse, however, and find yourself in Cork without a room, Bord Failte (Irish Tourist Board), will organise a reservation for a small fee. Their main office is on Grand Parade in the city centre. Phone (021) 4273251.

A cross section of accommodation is listed below. In an effort to keep things simple, the accommodation has been categorised as 'expensive', 'moderate' or 'budget'. Specific prices are not given as they often vary according to the timing of your stay - most of the selected hotels offer special deals, usually relating to weekend stays. Some of the city's guest houses offer rather more interesting accommodation than many of the hotels and a couple of the better ones are included in the moderate category.

Family-run B&B's form the bedrock of budget accommodation, costing around £25 per person sharing, but most are located in the suburbs of the city. Bookings can be made directly or through the Tourist Board. If you are looking for something cheap but close to the city centre, hostels offer a realistic alternative now that they have shaken off their down-at-heel image. Some have conventional bedrooms but most offer clean and comfortable dorm-style rooms with shared bathrooms. Price normally depends on how many are sharing, but rates are typically around £10 per person per night.

During the summer months from the middle of June through to the middle of September, it is possible to book university accommodation at UCC. This accommodation is well located and relatively cheap.

All Cork hotels are inspected by Bord Failte and each is given a star rating, from one to five stars, to reflect the standard of the accommodation and the facilities available. Guest houses, which tend to be less expensive than hotels, are graded on a similar system from one to four stars. The appropriate rating is listed below after the name of each establishment. The hotels and guest houses selected tend to provide rooms with en suite bathroom facilities as standard. For a more comprehensive list, a guide book called 'Be Our Guest' gives details of accommodation throughout Ireland which has been approved by the Tourist Board. The guide costs £3 and is available at all tourist offices.

EXPENSIVE

Arbutus Lodge Hotel* ** `13 L5`
Montenotte, Cork
Ph 021 4501237 Fax 021 4502893
Family owned hotel situated in Montenotte, once the preserve of Cork's merchant class, the Arbutus Lodge is an elegant townhouse built in 1802 with attractively terraced gardens which overlook the city and the River Lee. The hotel, which was once home to the Lord Mayor of Cork, has 20 bedrooms, each individually designed, and the hotel restaurant is among the best in Cork.

The Blue Haven* ** `22`
3-4 Pearse Street, KINSALE
Ph 021 4772209 Fax 021 4774268
One of the best known hotels in the county of Cork, the Blue Haven offers picture post card good looks, a location in the heart of Kinsale, an old world atmosphere, and a restaurant with a well earned reputation for delicious seafood.

Hayfield Manor*** ** `11 G8`
Perrott Avenue, Cork
Ph 021 431 5600 Fax 021 431 6839
Luxury five star hotel situated in 2 acres of mature gardens next door to UCC, about a mile from the centre of town. The hotel was built as recently as 1996 but it successfully conveys the feel of an old country manor. Facilities include a swim-

The Imperial Hotel on South Mall

ming pool and fitness suite.

Imperial Hotel*** `12 H7`
South Mall, Cork
Ph 021 4274040 Fax 021 4275375
Historic hotel which has enjoyed its city centre location since 1813. Michael Collins spent his last night at the hotel and the suite he stayed in still bears his name. The Imperial is only a couple of minutes walk from many of Cork's finest shops, restaurants and bars, although the hotel bar, South's, and its restaurant, Lafayette's, are among the most popular in town. 98 bedrooms.

Jury's Hotel**** `11 F7`
Western Road, Cork
Ph 021 4276622 Fax 021 4274477
Situated on the banks of the River Lee, about five minutes walk from the city centre. The 1970's architecture at Jury's is not terribly inspiring but the facilities ensure a comfortable stay. 185 bedrooms, expansive gardens which overlook the river, two restaurants and a bar.

Metropole Hotel*** `12 J6`
MacCurtain Street, Cork
Ph 021 450 8122 Fax 021 450 6450
Large city centre hotel which looks a lot better from the front than it does from behind. Conveniently located for the train station. Facilities include an indoor leisure centre with heated swimming pools, sauna, and a fitness suite.

Old Bank House**** `22`
11 Pearse Street, KINSALE
Ph 021 4774075 Fax 021 4774296
A former branch of the Munster & Leinster Bank which has been transformed into an elegant Georgian guesthouse with 17 bedrooms all individually furnished with antiques of the period.

MODERATE

Deasy's Long Quay House*** `22`
Long Quay, KINSALE

Ph 021 4774563 Fax 021 4774563
Attractive Georgian guesthouse which overlooks Kinsale harbour (rooms with a view cost a little extra). There are only seven bedrooms but all are tastefully furnished and offer terrific value for money.

Hotel Isaacs `12 J6`
48 MacCurtain Street, Cork
Ph 021 4500011 Fax 021 4506355
Situated five minutes walk from the city centre, the hotel offers both comfort and value as well as a convenient location near to both train and bus stations.

Jury's Cork Inn*** `12 J7`
Anderson's Quay, Cork
Ph 021 427 6444 Fax 021 427 6144
Jury's Inns are based on a fixed room rate format which the company is currently exporting to several British cities. The Cork Inn is centrally located with 133 bedrooms, many of which offer views over the River Lee. All rooms can accommodate up to three adults or two adults and two children. Breakfast is not included in the price but all rooms en suite with colour TV, telephone and tea/coffee making facilities and the hotel has a restaurant and bar.

Kieran's Folkhouse Inn*** `22`
Guardwell, KINSALE
Ph 021 4772382 Fax 021 4774085
Attractive 250 year old country inn with 27 bedrooms, bar, a restaurant which is a member of the Kinsale Gourmet Circle, and its own nightclub to boot! Kieran's offer some very good deals which include accommodation and an evening meal in the restaurant.

Lotamore House**** `14 N6`
Tivoli, Cork
Ph 021 4822344 Fax 021 4822219
Georgian guesthouse set in 4 acres of gardens overlooking the harbour and Blackrock Castle. About 10

The Blue Haven Hotel in Kinsale

minutes drive from the centre of Cork and within easy reach of many local amenities. 20 bedrooms.

Rochestown Park Hotel `21 N10`
Rochestown Road, Douglas, Cork
Ph 021 489 2233 Fax 021 489 2178
Situated on the south side of the city about 3 miles from the centre of town, the hotel facilities include a health & leisure centre with heated swimming pool. 115 bedrooms.

BUDGET

DeansHall `12 H7`
Phone (021) 4312623
DeansHall university accommodation is located opposite St Fin Barre's Cathedral at Crosse's Green. Available mid-June to mid-September.

Isaacs Hostel `12 J6`
48 MacCurtain St, Cork
Ph 021 4500011 Fax 021 4506355
63 rooms. Next to Hotel Isaacs.

Kinlay House (Hostel) `12 H6`
Shandon, Cork
Ph 021 4508966 Fax 021 4506927
Mixture of four and two bedded rooms and with some self catering accommodation.

The Crawford Municipal Art Gallery on Emmet Place

Ballincollig Gunpowder Mills
Ballincollig, Co Cork
Phone (021) 4874430
Situated on the banks of the River Lee about 5 miles southwest of Cork on the N22, the Royal Gunpowder Mills were established in 1794 and produced huge quantities of gunpowder for the British Army until they closed in 1903. A heritage centre has been opened on the 130 acre site to detail the history of the mills and the production process.

Bishop Lucey Park `12 H7`
Grand Parade, Cork
Just inside the park gates is a section of the old city walls which were destroyed during the Williamite siege of 1690.

Blackrock Castle `15 Q6`
Blackrock, Cork
Phone (021) 4357414
Situated on the banks of the river, only a mile from the city centre, the castle was rebuilt in 1830 after the original fortification was destroyed by fire. The building is now used as a banqueting hall, restaurant and bar. Open Tues-Sun

Blarney Castle
Blarney, Co Cork
The village of Blarney, which is situated about 5 miles northwest of Cork on the R617, offers plenty of scope if you are shopping for handcrafted goods, but the thousands of tourists who flock here come primarily to kiss the famous Stone of Eloquence' which is sit-

uated just below the battlements in the remains of Blarney Castle. The legend dates back to Elizabethan times when the castle was owned by Dermot McCarthy, Lord of Blarney who was notorious for failing to fulfil his agreements with the Queen. It was said that he was able to 'talk the noose off his neck' and, to this day, anyone kissing the Blarney Stone is said to be similarly endowed with the gift of eloquent and persuasive speech. Visitors can also take a tour of Blarney Castle House, a Scottish baronial mansion with attractive gardens.

Butter Exchange `12 H6`
John Redmond St, Cork
During the 18th and 19th centuries, Cork was one of the most important ports in Europe for the export of dairy products. The hub of this trade was the **Butter Exchange** which opened in 1770 in order to grade butter before it was exported around the world. The exchange closed in 1924 but part of the building has been reopened in recent years as the **Shandon Crafts Centre.**

Christ the King Church `12 J8`
Evergreen Road, Cork
Designed in the 1930's by Irish-American architect, Barry Byrne, the most striking feature is the cubist figure of Christ crucified with his arms spread above the twin doors at the entrance. The front of the church offers a panoramic view of the city.

City Hall `12 J7`
Albert Quay, Cork
Probably the most prominent building in Cork, the city hall was opened in 1936 to replace a previous building on the same site which was destroyed by fire in

1920 during the War of Independence.

Cobh

Following a visit by Queen Victoria in 1849, Cobh was renamed Queenstown before reverting to its original name in 1922. The town sits on a large island in Cork Harbour, about 15 miles southeast of Cork City, but it is connected to the mainland by roads and bridges. The harbour is one of the largest and safest any-where in the world and it has a long history of handling the largest passenger liners afloat. Cobh is an attractive Victorian town, built on the slope of a hill which looks out to Haulbowline and Spike Island, formerly the base of the Irish Naval Service. St Colman's Cathedral, with its car-illon of 47 bells, sits in pride of place at the top of the hill looking down onto the town below. The history of Cobh and its links to shipping and emigration and are explained in an interesting exhibi-tion called **The Queenstown Story** which is housed in the restored Victorian railway station (Phone 021 4813591. *Opening Times: Mon-Sun 10am-6pm. Admission £3.50 per adult).* An audio visual presentation and var-ious exhibits trace the story of the 2.5 million adults and children who emigrated from Ireland via Cobh, leaving on an assortment of 'coffin ships', convict ships, steamers and great ocean liners. Cobh was the last port of call for the Titanic which sank on her maiden voyage, and the Lusitania was sunk nearby by a German submarine in 1915 with the loss of 1198 lives. This action brought America into the Great War and the quayside memorial to the vic-tims reflects the fact that many of

Grand Parade with Cork City Tourist Office in the foreground

them were buried in Cobh, in the old churchyard of Clonmel.

Cork Archives Institute (C.A.I.)
South Main St, Cork `12 H7`

The Institute is housed in Christ Church, built in 1726 on the site of a mediaeval church destroyed in the 1690 siege. Founded in 1970 and funded jointly by Cork Corporation, Cork County Council and University College, the Institute collects and pre-serves public and private records and documents relating to the his-tory of Cork City and county. Search room services are avail-able by appointment only, and one weeks notice is usually required. *Opening Hours: Tues-Fri 10am-1pm & 2.30pm-5pm.*

Cork City Gaol `11 F7`
Sunday's Well, Cork
Phone (021) 4305022

The gaol no longer receives any prisoners but visitors are greeted with an audio visual exhibition which depicts what life was like for 19th century prisoners and gaolers. The old prison governor's residence houses an additional attraction, the **Radio**

Museum Experience which explains the history of Irish radio broadcasting and the impact that the invention of radio has had on our lives. *Open Daily: March-Oct 9.30am-6pm; Nov-Feb 10am-5pm. Admission £3.50 per adult for each exhibition*

Cork City Library `12 H7`
Grand Parade

Opening Times: Tues-Sat 10am-1pm & 2pm-5.30pm

Beamish Brewery on Sth Main Street

The beautiful coastline of west Cork just outside Baltimore

Cork Lough `12 G8`
Lough Road, Cork

Situated in a residential suburb of town, about a mile southwest of the city centre, The Lough is a large lake with an island which is home to a wide variety of birds including swans, ducks and moorhens.

Cork Public Museum `11 F7`
Fitzgerald Park
Phone (021) 4270679

The museum is housed in an attractive Georgian house which is surrounded 18 acres of parkland. The museum focuses mainly on social and political history with additional exhibits featuring the city's trades and crafts: silver, glassware, and lacework. A recent £2m extension has doubled the amount of exhibition space and created of a state of the art temporary exhibition gallery and a purpose-built research room where visitors can examine, handle and study artefacts and documents from the museum's collections. *Opening Times: Mon-Fri 11am-1pm & 2.15pm-5pm (until 6pm June-Aug); Sun 3pm-5pm. Admission is free except on Sundays when it costs £1.50*

Cork Vision Centre `12 H6`
St Peter's Church
North Main Street, Cork
Phone (021) 4279925

The centre, which is housed in a deconsecrated church dating back to 1788, hosts an exhibition promoting the city's past, present, and future plans for development. Exhibits include a 1:500 scale model of the city, a photographic perspective and a specially commissioned film on Cork's growth and development. *Opening Times: Tues-Sat 10am-5pm*

Court House `12 H7`
Washington Street, Cork

Built in 1835, the court house is one of the finest pieces of architecture in the city with an impressive Corinthian facade.

Crawford Art Gallery `12 G7`
Emmet Place, Cork
Phone (021) 4273377

The gallery, which is named after its founding benefactor William Horatio Crawford, started life in 1724 as the Custom House at a time when the street outside was the King's Dock. The building later became the Royal Cork Institution and then a school of design. W H Crawford funded an extension of the building in 1884 and further refurbishment is ongoing at the time of writing. The Crawford houses a collection of 19th and 20th century works by Irish artists such as Jack Yeats, Paul Henry and William Conor. Other exhibits include a collection of classical casts presented to the future King George IV by Pope Pius in 1818. The gallery also runs a programme of temporary exhibitions, featuring the work of Irish and international artists. *Opening Times: Mon-Sat 10am-5pm. Admission is free*

Dunkathel House
Glanmire, Co Cork
Phone (021) 4821014

Situated just outside Glanmire,

about 4 miles northeast of Cork, Dunkathel is a fine Georgian house built in 1790 for Abraham Morris, a wealthy Cork merchant. The staircase is built of Bath stone, many of the rooms have Adam fireplaces, and the house is furnished with antiques of the Georgian period including a cast of Canova's The Three Graces. *Opening Times: mid-May to mid-Oct Wed-sun 2pm-6pm*

Elizabeth Fort   `12 H8`
off Barrack Street, Cork
Built in the late 16th century during the reign of Elizabeth I, the fort is now used as a police station but parts of it remain open to the public and fine views of the city are available from its walls.

English Market   `12 H7`
Enter from Princes Street, St Patrick's Street or Grand Parade
Even if you are allergic to shopping, you should pop into the English Market and sample the colour and vitality of the place. Established in 1610, the current building dates back to 1786 since when it has been providing the city with fresh fish, meat, fruit and veg, not to mention the chance to catch up on a bit of people watching.

Father Matthew
One of Cork's best known landmarks is the statue of Father Theobald Matthew, 19th century Apostle of Temperance, which stands at the end of St Patrick's St, near to St Patrick's Bridge. His national crusade to persuade people to give up the drink is marked not only by the statue but also by Father Matthew Memorial Church which is situated on Father Matthew Quay. The

A pot still in the grounds of the Old Midleton Distillery

church is notable for its elegance and a fine stained glass window dedicated to Daniel O'Connell.

Fitzgerald Park   `11 F7`
Mardyke Walk, Cork
Situated by the banks of the river, the 18 acre park is attractively landscaped and offers a peaceful oasis less than a mile from the centre of town.

Fota Wildlife Park
Carrigtwohill, Co Cork
Phone (021) 4812678
Situated just off the N25, about six miles east of Cork city, Fota Wildlife Park is set in 70 acres of open countryside. The attractive setting is home to over 90 exotic species from 5 continents, and many of the animals are free to wander throughout the park. Giraffes, cheetahs and zebras are among the animals on show, but a strong emphasis is put on conservation and breeding of endangered species. Facilities include free playgrounds, a wildlife train, picnic areas, arboretum & gar-

dens, restaurant, gift shop and a video show. Animal feeding times are early morning and late afternoon. *Opening Times: From mid-March to end of September Mon-Sat 10am-6pm, Sun 11am-6pm; open only at weekends during the rest of the year. Admission £4.80 per adult, £2.70 per child*

Jameson Heritage Centre
Midleton, Co Cork
Phone (021) 4613594
Located about 12 miles east of Cork City on the road to Waterford, a visit to the **Old Midleton Distillery** takes the form of a guided tour which begins with an audio-visual presentation, followed by a walk through the historic mills, malting houses, corn stores, warehouses and stillhouses which all played their part in the whiskey making process. Whiskey production now takes place at a new plant next door, but the original distilling equipment remains in place in the old distillery and exhibits include the largest pot still in the world

Boats in Kinsale marina

which has a capacity of 32,000 gallons. The tour finishes in the Jameson Bar with an Irish Whiskey tasting session. Other facilities include a gift shop. *Opening Times: March-October 10am-6pm (last tour 4.30pm); November-Feb 2 tours daily Mon-Fri 12pm & 3pm, Sat & Sun 2pm & 4pm. Admission charge.*
Nb **The Clean Slate,** which is situated at the entrance to the distillery, is one of the best restaurants in the county of Cork. Phone (021) 4633655.

Kinsale `22`
Kinsale gets its name from the Irish, *Cionn Saile*, meaning tide head. Situated about 18 miles southwest of Cork City, the town used to be an important naval port but is best known today as one of the country's oldest and prettiest seaside towns, and for its reputation as 'the gourmet capital of Ireland'. As well as great scope for eating and drinking (see pages 53-64), there is plenty to do and see in and around the town including several buildings dating back to medieval times.

In 1601 Ireland joined forces with Spain against the English, and the Spanish fleet anchored at Kinsale before being defeated at the Battle of Kinsale which led to the end of the Gaelic clan system and 'The Flight of the Earls' following the failed rebellion against Elizabeth I.

There's a good view of Kinsale from **Charles Fort** which was built in the reign of Charles II

as a military base on the site of an earlier Norman fortification. The fort, which housed an army garrison up until 1922, is open to the public from April to October. The other side of the narrow entrance to Kinsale harbour is guarded by **James Fort** which was built in 1602. A few miles further out of town is the **Old Head of Kinsale** which offers some spectacular cliff scenery and a new championship golf course. The nearby resort of **Garretstown** benefits from good sandy beaches.

St Multose Church, which dates back to 1190, marks the centre of the medieval town and many of its original features still survive including inscriptions in Norman French. The other important medieval building which still remains is Desmond Castle on Cork Street. It was built around 1500 by Maurice Bacach Fitzgerald, Earl of Desmond whose family controlled Kinsale until the 1580's when their lands were confiscated following a failed rebellion. The castle was turned into a prison in the 17th

Father Matthew Church

century and used mostly for prisoners of war which explains why it became known as the French Prison. Since 1997 the castle has housed the International Museum of Wine which traces the history of the castle, Kinsale's development as a wine port, and Ireland's links to the global wine trade which date back to the mass emigration of the 17th, 18th and 19th centuries. **The Old Courthouse**, on Market Square, was built around 1600 and is now home to the **Regional Museum.** All of these attractions are marked on the map of Kinsale on page 22.

National Monument   `12 H7`
Grand Parade, Cork
Monument to Irish patriots who died between 1798 and 1867.

Red Abbey 12 H7   `12 H7`
Red Abbey Street
The square tower is all that remains of a 12th century Augustinian Priory which used to stand just outside the city walls. During the siege of 1690, the Duke of Marlborough mounted a cannon on the tower in order to pound the walls and batter the city into submission. The medieval tower is the oldest piece of architecture in the city.

Riverstown House
Glanmire, Co Cork
Phone (021) 4821205
Situated at Glanmire, about four miles out of Cork on the road to Dublin, the house was built in 1602 and is famed for the 1730's plasterwork of the Swiss-Italian Lafranchini brothers. This work was commissioned by the Archbishop of Cork, Dr Jemmett Browne, and the house remained in his family until the early 20th century.

SS Peter & Paul Church   `12 H7`
Situated off St Patrick's Street, the church was designed by the younger Pugin and built in Gothic style in 1866.

St Anne's Shandon   `12 H6`
Church Street, Cork
St Anne's is an Anglican church built between 1722 and 1726 to replace one destroyed during the Williamite siege of 1690. It is best known for its bells and its bell tower which has two faces built in white limestone and the other two in red sandstone, topped off with an 11 foot salmon which acts as a weather vane. It costs £1.50 to climb the tower and enjoy the view over the city, but the price includes an opportunity to ring the 8 bells which were cast in Gloucestershire in 1750. By selecting the appropriate punchcard, the population below can enjoy your rendition of anything from Ave Maria to Danny Boy! *Opening Times: Mon-Sat 10am-5pm*

St Anne's Shandon

St Fin Barre's Cathedral

St Fin Barre's Cathedral   `12 G7`
Bishop Street, Cork
Phone (021) 4322993
Built between 1867 and 1879 by wealthy Church of Ireland merchants, the cathedral stands on the site where St Fin Barre founded his monastery and university back in the 6th century. The current building was constructed in French Gothic style in white limestone with three towering spires which dominate the city skyline. The stone carving at the entrance sets the standard for some magnificent craftsmanship within, which includes a beautifully painted and gilded apse ceiling and some wonderful stained glass. The cannonball hanging south of the altar is said to have been fired at the tower of the previous church during the siege of 1690. The life of St Fin Barre is celebrated annually on the 25th September. A restoration project to mark the new millennium is currently under way and, once the target figure of £5 million has been raised and spent, the cathedral will have had a new roof,

St Mary's Dominican Church

restorative work will have been carried out on the stained glass windows, and an Interpretive Centre will have been added underground in the forecourt of the cathedral. The cathedral is open 10am-5pm and guided tours are available.

St Mary's Dominican Church
Pope's Quay, Cork   `12 H6`
Completed in 1839 with an impressive classical facade which

faces directly onto the river. Home to the 'miraculous' statuette of Our Lady of Graces.

St Mary's pro-Cathedral `12 H6`
Cathedral Street, Cork
Catholic cathedral, begun in 1808, and noted for its carvings. The presbytery contains records of baptisms and marriages from 1748.

Tourist Information Office
Grand Parade, Cork   `12 H7`
Phone (021) 4273251
Mine of useful information and a good place to sort out accommodation and touring requirements.

Triskel Arts Centre   `12 H7`
Tobin Street, Cork
Phone 4272022
If you are expecting the arts scene in Cork to be provincial by nature, Triskel will soon persuade you otherwise with its avante garde programme of art, cinema, and live music. There are two gallery spaces which tend to concentrate on exhibitions of contemporary art, an arthouse cinema which screens a mixture of foreign language films and cult classics, and

a live music venue which hosts performances of jazz, classical and rock. An added bonus is the Yumi Yuki Club upstairs, a sushi & sake cafe bar which is open day and night, before during and after performances in the centre. *Gallery Opening Times: Mon-Sat 10am-5.30pm*

University College Cork
College Road   `11 F8`
Phone (021) 4903000
Established in 1849, when it was known as The Queen's University, UCC stands in very attractive grounds which offer some fine views over the city below. University life revolves around a Tudor Gothic quadrangle that would not look out of place in Oxford or Cambridge, which probably explains why it was used in the filming of Chariots of Fire. The Honan Chapel, which is modelled on the 12th century Cormac's Chapel at Cashel, has an impressive interior with some beautiful stained glass windows designed by Harry Clarke and Sarah Purser.

The main quadrangle at University College Cork

Cork, like the rest of Ireland, is proud of its artistic tradition and the arts have been going from strength to strength in recent years thanks to considerable refurbishment and investment in new venues, and continuing financial support from public and private sectors.

A multi million pound redevelopment of the Opera House is currently under way which will add significantly to the city's artistic stock, but the cultural highlight of the year remains the Guinness Cork Jazz Festival which normally lasts for a long weekend at the end of October when an array of international performers come to town.

If you are planning a night out at the theatre, cinema or a performance of live music or comedy *The Examiner's* entertainment section is a good place to start. Alternatively, pick up a free copy of *The List* which is published fortnightly and can be picked up from many pubs and other venues around town.

THEATRE

Cork Arts Theatre   `12 H6`
7 Knapps Square, Cork
Phone (021) 4508398

Everyman Palace Theatre
15 MacCurtain Street   `12 J6`
Phone (021) 4501673
The Everyman started life as a cinema but is now one of Cork's leading arts venues, staging plays by both Irish and international playwrights, before transforming into a late night club venue once the night's performance has finished.

Firkin Crane   `12 H6`
Dominick St, Cork
Phone (021) 4507487
Theatre in what was once the weighing station for the Butter Exchange. Programme of drama, dance and music which is often of an experimental nature.

Granary Theatre   `12 G7`
Dyke Parade, Cork
Phone (021) 4904275
Home to UCC Dramat, the university's theatre company, who stage a wide body of work including plays by new writers as well as the classics. Every Tuesday is a "Pay What You Can" night when you choose your own ticket price.

Half Moon Theatre   `12 H7`
Half Moon Street, Cork
Phone (021) 4274308
Situated at the back of the Opera House, the Half Moon is a versatile venue which stages theatre, live music and comedy as well as acting as a night club.

OPERA

Cork Opera House may be the city's leading arts venue but it is not what you might expect. In fact, from the outside, it might be mistaken for a 1960's multi storey car park! All this set to change, however, as the Opera House is currently undergoing a multi million pound redevelopment which will give it a more contemporary look. Gone will be the square corners in favour of flowing curves and a new glass frontage.

The Opera House is home to **Opera Cork** who host performances and concerts throughout the year featuring both local talent and international artists. Slightly further afield, about 100 miles in fact, **Wexford Festival Opera** takes place annually during the autumn (19th Oct - 5th Nov 2000). The distance is worth travelling for what has become a world renowned festival with an international programme which usually includes three major productions and over 40 other events. Telephone bookings can be made on (053) 22144.

Cork Opera House   `12 H6`
Emmet Place, Cork
Phone (021) 4270022

MUSIC

Music is very close to Irish hearts and souls and it is almost impossible to visit Cork without experiencing a musical encounter of one sort or another.

Traditional Irish music remains very popular with locals and visitors alike while Ireland also has a strange love affair with country & western music, but it is in the field of rock and popular music that the Irish have made their presence felt on the world stage in recent years with bands such as U2, The Cranberries, Boyzone and The Corrs, and individuals such as Van Morrison, Bob Geldof, Sinéad O'Connor and Enya, to name but a few.

It will come as no surprise to learn that Cork pubs provide the main platform for local bands and musicians. There are dozens of such venues and many of them are listed in the Pubs section on pages 53 to 58. A good choice of rock, jazz, folk and blues is usually on offer. For lovers of jazz, the annual highlight is **Guinness Cork Jazz Festival** (Oct 27th-30th 2000). Now in its 23rd year, the festival offers a long weekend of non-stop jazz performed by an international array of musicians from all five continents. Major events tend to sell out very quickly but it is possible to book in advance through the Opera House (021 4270022). If you are planning to visit for the duration of the

City Limits music and comedy venue on Coburg Street

festival, you should book your hotel room well in advance. You can visit the festival web site at www.corkjazzfestival.com or phone (021) 4278979 for more information.

For lovers of choir music, Cork International Choral Festival takes place in April/May. For more information, phone (021) 4308308

COMEDY

Ireland has produced a rich crop of stand-up comedians in recent years including Ardal O'Hanlon, Sean Hughes, Dylan Moran, Ed Byrne, and Tommy Tiernan, the most recent of several Irish winners of the prestigious Perrier Award at the Edinburgh Festival. It has to be said though that most of these acts were actually blooded on the London comedy circuit, but Cork has a couple of good venues of its own which are helping to keep the production line rolling, and Kinsale manages to attract some top quality acts dur-

ing the height of the tourist season.

The **Half Moon Theatre** (see details on page 47) stages comedy on Tuesday nights while **City Limits** on Coburg Street (phone 021 4501206) also stages regular comedy nights with well known acts often topping the bill.

CINEMA

With the help of tax incentives provided by the government, the Irish film industry continues to go from strength to strength, with many notable successes such as The Commitments, Brave Heart and Saving Private Ryan. Cinema attendances have soared in recent years and the Irish now go to the 'flicks' more often than anybody else in Europe. The number of screens in and around Cork continues to rise with the advent of the multiplex.

HQ for arthouse cinema is **Cinematek** at the **Triskel Arts Centre**. Cinematek is technically a members only club for the over-

18's, but in effect you simply pay a pound to be a member for a week and members are entitled to buy tickets for up to two guests. Its status means that uncertified films are occasionally screened as the club does not have to submit all of its films to the censor.

The highlight of the cinematic year is the **Murphy's Cork Film Festival** which takes place in October and is now in its 44th year. The festival attracts entries from around the world and has premiered many successful films over the years. For more information, phone (021) 4271711 or visit the festival web site on www.corkfilmfest.org

Capitol Cineplex 12 H7
Grand Parade, Cork
Phone (021) 4278 777
6 screens

Cinema World 20 M11
Douglas, Cork
Phone (021) 4895959
5 screens

Cinematek 12 H6
Triskel Arts Centre
Tobin Street, Cork
Phone (021) 4272022
Cinematek screenings are open to members and their guests. Membership costs £1 for a week, £5 for a year, and must be taken out 15 minutes before screening. A member can buy tickets for two guests per screening.

Kino Cinema 12 G7
Washington Street, Cork
(021) 4271571

Reel Picture
Times Square
Ballincollig, Co Cork
Phone (021) 4876300
6 screens

ANGLING

South west Ireland is an angler's delight with a beautiful coastline, and miles of rivers and loughs teeming with salmon, trout, bream, rudd, pike and tench. Kinsale is a popular spot for sea anglers, and boats are available for hire with skipper on a daily basis. The local speciality is blue shark which arrives about mid-June but there is a wide variety of other species which can be caught all year round. For more information, contact the **South Western Regional Fisheries Board** which is based in Macroom. Phone (026) 41221.

GAELIC GAMES

Gaelic football and hurling are Ireland's two national sports, and both have their headquarters in Dublin at Croke Park which is Ireland's finest sports stadium. Cork's main venue is Pairc Ui Chaoimh.

Kinsale Harbour - a haven for sailing and angling enthusiasts

Gaelic football most resembles Australian Rules football, although the Irish play with a round ball. Ireland's 32 counties compete for a place in the All Ireland Final which takes place at Croke Park on the third Sunday in September in front of 80,000 spectators.

To say that hurling resembles a combination of hockey and lacrosse hardly does the game justice. The All Ireland hurling final is staged on the first Sunday in September, also at Croke Park.

Cork club and county sides have acquired many championships over the years and remain among the heavyweights where both games are concerned.

GOLF

Unlike many other countries, golf is not seen as an elitist game in Ireland. There are about a dozen courses within half an hour of the centre of Cork and several of these are of championship standard. There are three courses in and around Kinsale, including a new course at the Old Head of Kinsale which asks some very tough golfing questions while providing spectacular sea views to compensate if you can't come up with the answers. Closer to Cork is Fota Island, only 10 minutes drive from the centre of town. Fota feels quite American in its design and it is due to host the Irish Open in both 2001 and 2002. Cork has courses to suit players of all abilities and green fees tend not to be prohibitively expensive. A few of the better ones are listed below. All are private clubs but visitors are welcome, especially during the week, although it is advisable to phone beforehand.

Fota Island
Phone (021) 4883710
Tough, par 72, championship

course situated about 10 minutes drive on the N25 from the centre of Cork. Sister course to the more famous Mount Juliet Resort in Kilkenny. Fota will host the Irish Open in 2001 and 2002.

Kinsale Golf Club
Farrangalway & Ringenane
The club has two courses in and around Kinsale, a relatively new 18 hole course at Farrangalway (phone 021 4774722) and a long established 9 holer at Ringenane (phone 021 4772197). Both offer a pleasant challenge and are well worth a visit. Farrangalway measures 6,609 yards and is a par 71, while Ringenane measures 5,332 yards and is situated on the slope of a hill which runs down to the banks of the Belgooly river estuary.

Little Island
Phone (021) 4353451
Situated about 5 miles east of Cork

City on the N25, Little Island is an attractive parkland course on the banks of Lough Mahon. At 6,065 metres and a par of 72, the course is of championship standard.

Harbour Point, Little Island
Phone (021) 4353094
Set among rolling hills overlooking Lough Mahon about 6 miles east of Cork City, this is a championship standard course measuring 6,063 metres with a par of 72. Covered 21 bay floodlit driving range is an added bonus.

Old Head of Kinsale
Phone (021) 4778444
One of the toughest and most spectacular courses in Ireland. The course is perched on a headland, surrounded by cliffs, with sea views on every hole. This part of the coast is often affected by sea fog, so it is advisable to phone before you arrive to check that conditions are clear.

HORSE RACING & RIDING

Ireland is famous throughout the world for producing thoroughbred race horses, which helps to explain why the Irish love to have a flutter on the outcome of a race.

Unfortunately for local punters, Cork Park Racecourse closed in 1916 but numerous hunter trials and point to points are held locally, and **Mallow's** spectacular racecourse is only 20 minutes drive from Cork City.

If you prefer riding horses to betting on them, **Hop Island Equestrian Centre** is conveniently located in Rochestown. Facilities include an indoor and outdoor arena as well as cross country riding. Phone (021) 4361277

RUGBY

Lansdowne Road in Dublin is the headquarters of the Irish Rugby Football Union and the home venue for all of Ireland's international matches. The highlight of the year is the Six Nations Championship which takes place from January to March when Ireland take on England, Scotland, Wales, France and Italy. Thousands of away fans invade Dublin for what is a great social occasion and, despite a conspicuous lack of Irish success, tickets are very difficult to acquire.

Munster, who contribute several players to the Irish team, have long enjoyed a reputation as giant killers with victories over the All Blacks and the Wallabies to their credit. The team recently missed out on further glory when they lost to Northampton by a single point in the final of the 2000 European Cup. Home games are played at Thomond Park in Limerick.

SAILING & WATERSPORTS

The south west coast of Ireland is one of the most popular yachting areas in Europe. The **Royal Cork Yacht Club**, based at **Crosshaven,** is the oldest sailing club in the world, dating back to 1720 when it was founded in Cobh. **Kinsale** is another important sailing centre with Blue Flag Marina facilities for visiting boats and yacht charter available from near the Trident Hotel. Sailing and windsurfing courses are on offer at **Oysterhaven,** south east of Kinsale.

SNOOKER & 10 PIN BOWLING

The Mardyke `12 G7`
Sheares Street, Cork
Phone (021) 4273000
11 snooker tables and 9 American pool tables forming part of this new entertainment complex.

Leisureplex `12 J6`
MacCurtain Street, Cork
Snooker, pool & ten pin bowling 24 hours a day.

SOCCER

For many years Irish soccer lived in the shadow of Gaelic sports until big Jack (Charlton) came from England, of all places, to manage the national side. Ten years of unprecedented success in the European Championships and the World Cup gripped the nation. Jack recently returned to his fishing rod and the team is currently being rebuilt by a new manager, Mick McCarthy. International matches are played at Lansdowne Road rugby stadium in Dublin and the headquarters of the Football Association of Ireland is at 80 Merrion Square - phone (01) 676 6864.

In Cork, Gaelic games still reign supreme, but Cork City, the local soccer team, did manage to win the League of Ireland for the first time in 1993 and have since added to that success by winning the Cup in 1998. League of Ireland games are normally played on Sundays but support for the local side is dwarfed by the passionate interest which Corkonians take in the English Premiership and 'local boys made good' such as Denis Irwin and Roy Keane.

SWIMMING

If you aren't afraid of cold water, there are plenty of beaches within easy reach of the city. If you are not feeling so hardy, one of the city's public swimming pools might be a more realistic alternative:

Leisureworld `10 B9`
Rossa Avenue, Cork
Phone (021) 4346505
Modern pool and gym complex with a busy programme of lessons and keep fit. Best to phone beforehand to make sure that the pool is available for public use.

A substantial student population inevitably influences shopping opportunities in any city, and Cork students go for the casual, street-orientated, budget look, and look pretty good on it too. Perhaps the city's continental links have promoted the exchange of some French chic for some Irish craic. 1970's style faded jeans and baggy Aran jumper wearers with Murphys-encrusted beards and moustaches are luckily in the decline.

For the *Oirish* tourist market there are mercifully scant pickings in Cork City but plenty in nearby Blarney. Dotted throughout the county there are various arts and crafts shops, usually attached to an individual artisan. Many are high quality, inventive, and a real find, but unfortunately some rely heavily on the 'hand made' tag synonymous with tat.

The relatively temperate climate, the spiritual connection with France, and the lack of the stag party scene associated with Dublin's Temple Bar makes going out in Cork both safe and great fun. Alcohol fuelled party goers still like to look their best, however, and if you intend joining them, a few fashion tips follow:

Fashion

Shopping in the **Merchant's Quay Centre**, the city's newest and largest shopping centre, may not mean you are making much of a fashion statement, but it does mean that you are canny enough to kit yourself out in this seasons gear for little cash at the likes of **O Japan, Extrovert, Storan**, or, if you are going for the classic cut, **Marks and Spencer**. A large branch of **Dunnes Stores** with fabulous value Irish linen and a new in house line to capture the young and hip market is a stalwart. This takes you onto the main thoroughfare of St Patrick Street with budget department stores **Roches** and **Penny's** and the usual English High Street multiples of **Monsoon**,

Roches Stores and Brown Thomas on busy St Patrick's Street

Warehouse, RiverIsland, Wallis, Body Shop, Vero Moda and **Benetton**, interlaced with a few tacky boutiques. **Bari** does stock the sort of clothes that feature in youf clubby magazines but with superior quality and style. **Quill's** is a quaint juxtaposition of mens formal wear, designer casual such as **Matinique**, young and trendy stock, and the aforementioned lumpy Aran sweaters. Similarly **Gentleman's Quarter** conjures up an image of a bygone era but is actually stocked with desirables from **Pepe, Firetrap, Kickers** and **FCUK**.

Nearby Oliver Plunkett Street has boutiques to entice the woman who has paid off her student loan a few years ago such as **Richard Allen, Betty Barclays** and **Carl Scarpa** where a stylish clothes range is in stock as well as the established shoe line. Young bodies can show themselves off at the French owned chain of **Morgans** and men can be gently coerced into looking their best in **Boss, Lacoste** or **Feraud** at **Saville's. Minihan's Chemists** will supply your prophylactic hangover needs before you stagger upstairs to the Hi-B.

Tucked just off Prince's Street is **Jive** if looking like a surfer in **Stussy** and **Quicksilver** is your thing (sun bleached blond hair and Cork induced sun tan optional). Another little corner of individuality is **Winthrop Arcade. Designer Fusion** has deliciously frothy and formal designer clothing whereas **Drop/Nuisance** sell men's and women's urban sport cottons to a live DJ beat. **Annie Brennan's** window displays jewellery from several different designers. Don't miss the enormous **Mahers Sports** store with suitably big name labels. Another sports shop is **Welch Sports** on Maylor Street. Nearby is **Delicato** where lovely and unusual clothes will make you part with substantial sums of money. Any clothes horse will tell you an outfit needs the right accessories and jewellery from **Equinox** will not let you down.

Cross to the other side of St Patrick's Street and you are in a little warren of attractive and funky streets. French Church Street has shops to suit all tastes, whether you want sophistication from **Monica John** or phat clothing from **Store. DV8** will make sure your need for

One of the many fresh food stalls at The English Market

funky footwear is met and **Shades** will supply the eyewear. **Cheapskate** will kit you out in the skate clothing that seems to be the young Corkonian staple style.

Neighbouring Academy Street's **Black Boot** carries on the urban sports theme, but if you like the crack of leather and heaving flesh between your legs then **The Tack Room** is for you. On Half Moon Street is the massive **Surf Shop** in the **Matthew Centre** but, if your taste is for impeccably cut, understated and elegant clothes, head for the unassailably chic **The Dressing Room** in Emmet Place. On St. Paul's Street feed your body beautiful at **The Natural Foods Health Store**, (and then sneak a patisserie at the Gingerbread House), before completing the groomed look by buying jewellery at **IMB** in Rory Gallagher Square. To crown it all, pay attention to your crown at **Toni & Guy's** or **D'arcy's Design,** both top hairdressing salons.

Near to the Triskel Arts Centre is **Time** which continues the skater/surfer theme by packing in clothes from the likes of **Hooch** and **Pash.** Quality jewellers such as **Keanes** and **Hilser & Sons** will always survive the vagaries of fashion. The mecca of all fashion stores, the platinum card paradise of pleasure, is **Brown Thomas Department Store** back on St. Patrick's Street - a personal favourite, although a lack of buying power means that more time is spent in the BT-owned **A Wear** across the road. A Wear stocks younger, up to the minute fashions with a designer collection that combines that smug knowledge that you are looking good and it hasn't cost the earth. The contemporary design section in Brown Thomas itself does replicate some of the clothes from A Wear, but its strength as a department store is not just the array of clothes, jewellery, furniture, perfumes etc., the chic interior, not even the fact that it is often good value, it is the pleasant atmosphere. Retail therapy requires the right attitude of the staff, the ambience for enjoyment and Brown Thomas gets my vote every time.

Interiors

Ireland may be breaking out in a rash of Spanish style hacienda bungalows, but good taste is to the fore at the **Meadows & Byrne** emporium on Academy Street which will fulfil all your interior design fantasies and has a decent cafe to boot. Close by on Emmet Place is the furniture store, **Marble & Lemon,** stuffed with a hotchpotch of quality and style.

Books

Cork city centre has a high concentration of major bookshops. The Irish heavyweight, **Easons,** has a branch on St Patrick's Street with a surprisingly trendy cafe. **Waterstones** with entrances on St Patrick's Street and Paul Street stocks a wide range but retains a strong emphasis on local culture. Also on Paul Street is the intriguing specialist shop called **Mainly Murder.** Another major outlet is **Mercier Bookstore** on nearby French Church St while **Connolly's Bookshop** on Rory Gallagher Place stocks new books as well as a wide range of second hand for those on a tight budget. The charming **Cork Bookshop** is on Carey's Lane.

Markets

The **English Market** on Princes Street is a must whether you are a local trying to buy the freshest and cheapest produce around or a tourist looking to soak up some atmosphere. Rather than have an English feel to it, the astounding olive, bread, and fish stalls bear testimony to Cork's standing as a port with strong trading links to coastal Europe. **Coal Quay Market** on Cornmarket Street is not in the league of continental flea markets but a rummage never goes amiss, although a genuine bargain find demands a fair degree of luck.

It seems that wherever you go in the world these days, an Irish pub is rarely far away. Ireland rightly has a reputation for great pubs and Cork certainly upholds this tradition. The pub represents the heart and soul of the city's social life and there are hundreds to choose from.

There are many historic pubs dotted mainly around the city centre, and a growing number of modern ones which reflect the growing trend for café bars. It is difficult in many cases to distinguish between pubs, clubs and bars as many of Cork's watering holes fit comfortably into all three categories. The list below tries to point you in the direction of some of the best but, if you feel strongly that any have been wrongly included or unfairly omitted, feel free to let us know (see page 2 for contact details).

Most of the pubs listed serve food and many stage live music. To find out who is playing when and where, pick up a copy of *The List,* a free guide to what's on which is published every fortnight and is available in many bars and cafes around town. Alternatively, buy a copy of Cork's daily newspaper, *The Examiner.*

Opening hours are NOT included in the listings below as they are often subject to extensions which can vary according to what's on, but there's usually little problem in getting hold of a late drink any night of the week. Pubs normally open their doors at 10.30am from

Stocking the bar at The Roundy

Monday to Saturday, and at 12.30pm on Sunday. Doors are closed from 2pm-4pm on Sundays, but you will often be able to stay on during these hours as long as you are in before 2pm. Closing time is 11.30pm from May until September, and 11pm in winter and on Sundays. Half an hour drinking up time is allowed after closing.

When it comes to drinking up, stout reigns supreme in Cork where two local brews, Murphy's and Beamish take the fight to the Dublin heavyweight, Guinness. Many Corkonians spend much of their life in search of the perfect pint and everybody has their own opinion as to which of the three is the best. Where the Japanese have their tea ceremony, Irish barmen perform their own ritual when pouring a pint of the black stuff but, like all good things in life, it is usually worth waiting for.

Cork is nothing if not compact and life for the pub dweller is made even easier by the fact that many of the most popular bars are concentrated within the city centre. If you are an advocate of the pub crawl, then relax in the knowledge that you won't have far to walk and feel free to work your way through the list below!

An Spailpín Fánac   `12 H7`
28 South Main Street
Phone (021) 4277949

Situated across the road from Murphy's Brewery, An Spailpín Fánac is one of the best known and most frequented pubs in town. The stone floors, bare brick walls lined with memorabilia, the lovely old bar and the maze of different rooms and snugs all combine to make this among the best of the traditional Irish bars in Cork city. This is no secret, however, and come night time the place is

Bodega on on Cornmarket Street

packed to the gunnels with customers from near and far who come to enjoy the regular sessions of live traditional music.

Bar Rumba   `12 H7`
Tuckey Street

Modern bar cum club, with a slightly OTT line in interior design, which attracts a young crowd who like to party late into the night.

Barry's   `12 H8`
Barrack Street

Barrack Street is a steep hill which starts its climb close to St Fin Barre's Cathedral. Barry's, which is half way up on the right hand side, is an outstanding example of a good Cork local. The bar is plain and simple, the atmosphere is cosy and relaxed, and the landlord is happy to engage in chat about any subject under the sun. Word has it that Moss Keane, the father of Manchester United's Roy Keane, sometimes pops in for a pint. Moss, apparently, is better known to the locals as Sterling Moss due to the amount of English money which he carries around in his pocket these days!

The Grand Circle on Emmet Place

A traditional Irish bar, simply but tastefully fitted out with the possible exception of the IKEA spotlights used to illuminate the bar. Apart from that, the feeling is that of a bar from yesteryear, a place to savour a decent pint and enjoy a bit of craic. And if you prefer the outdoor air, the rear courtyard serves as a small beer garden.

Dan Lowrey's Tavern `12 J6`
13 MacCurtain Street
Phone (021) 4505071
Classic 19th century bar with an impressive frontage of stained glass which started life as a church window in Killarney. The interior is long, narrow and totally wood panelled which helps to generate a cosy atmosphere. Good value lunch and dinner with seafood featuring as the speciality of the house.

Fred Zepplins `12 H7`
8 Parliament Street, Cork
Phone (021) 4273500
Apart from the endless 'happy hours', the main attraction of this 'alternative rock bar' is the daily diet of live music.

Bodega `12 H7`
46-49 Cornmarket Street
Phone (021) 4272878
To describe it as 'Dublin chic comes to Cork' would be unfair to Bodega, because this is a bar with sufficient self confidence to bear comparison with the very best on offer in the capital, and anywhere else for that matter - the sort of place where they ask you if you want your sandwich on black olive bread or ciabatta.

Housed in an old warehouse, the interior is cavernous, yet warm. The stone walls have been painted cream and are lined with original artwork, potted palms sprout among the tables and comfortable velvet sofas, and massive lamp

shades hang down from the open rafters. The bar is dominated by four towering mirrors which stretch up to a mezzanine floor above. By day, the Bodega is a great spot to chill out while enjoying a sandwich or something more substantial from the lunch menu. The upstairs restaurant opens at night, while the main bar is densely populated with hip clientele from Cork and out of town. Resident DJ's entertain in the upstairs bar every Thursday and Sunday and there are live jazz sessions downstairs on Sundays.

Counihan's Bar `12 J7`
Pembroke Street
Phone (021) 4277850

Grand Circle `12 H6`
Emmet Place
Phone (021) 4274546
Situated across the road from the Crawford Art Gallery, The Grand Circle is a traditional local which must, single handedly, keep the local taxidermy industry going judging by the assortment of stuffed wildlife on display.

Hairy Lemon `12 H7`
Oliver Plunkett Street
Phone (021) 4278678
As you might discern from the name and the frontage, this is a bar with a certain attitude. Step inside and you will discover a single roomed bar with few creature

comforts, but a good soundtrack, decent cocktails and endless 'happy hours' more than atone.

Half Moon Theatre `12 H7`
Half Moon Street
Phone (021) 4270022
Located at the rear of the Opera House, the Half Moon is a venue for theatre, live music and comedy (every Tuesday night). And just for good measure it is also one of the best clubs in town, featuring regular soul and salsa nights.

Havana Brown's `12 G7`
Washington Street
Late night clubbing venue.

Henchy's `13 K6`
40 St Luke's Cross
Phone (021) 4507833
Getting to Henchy's requires a fifteen minute hike uphill from the centre of town, but the effort is rewarded with a beautifully unspoilt Victorian pub where change has been implemented with a subtlety which has not undermined the old world charm of the place. Less touristy than many of the city centre pubs, Henchy's offers comfort and space aplenty, with lots of nice touches to interest the roving eye.

The Hi-B `12 H7`
Above Minahan's Chemist
108 Oliver Plunkett Street
Phone (021) 4272758
The Hibernian Bar, to give it its full name, is one of Cork's drinking institutions, especially when 'himself', Brian the landlord, is behind the bar. It's a little difficult to find, being located at the top of a dark flight of stairs, above Minahan's Chemist, on the corner of Winthrop Street and Oliver Plunkett Street. The bar itself is a single room with a lino floor and simple but comfortable furnish-

ings, all slightly frayed at the edges. The clientele is a mix of local characters and tourists from around the globe, with the former holding court mainly from the seats at the bar.

Le Chateau Bars/Reidy's
93 St. Patrick Street `12 H7`
Phone (021) 4270370
Established in 1793 at a time when Patrick Street was a waterway and boats were tied up outside, the front bar has a comfortable Victorian interior while the back bar is equally comfy but more modern in feel.

The Lobby `12 J7`
1 Union Quay
Phone (021) 4311113
Situated on the river, just across the road from the City Hall, The Lobby is one of the top venues in town for live traditional music. The downstairs bar is a small, no-frills affair which hosts free sessions several times a week. This is a great attraction for tourists and the place can sound like a branch of the US embassy at times. An assortment of bands, from both near and far, perform upstairs in front of a paying audience.

The Lobby on Union Quay

The Long Valley Bar `12 H7`
10 Winthrop Street
Phone (021) 4272144
The word 'institution' can be over used when describing bars but the Long Valley definitely falls into this category. At the time of writing the bar is undergoing a few improvements but the end product will hopefully retain the quirky, old world charm which the Long Valley has been renowned for since 1842. The staff are first rate, there are plenty of local characters among the customers, and the sandwiches are the best in town. Traditional music sessions Tuesday-Thursday.

Tardis-like dimensions at The Old Oak on Oliver Plunkett Street

Victorian splendour at Reidy's

Old Oak `12 H7`
113 Oliver Plunkett St
Phone (021) 4276165
Should perhaps be known as Doctor Who's, due to the tardis-like dimensions within. The fit-out is recent but designed along traditional lines with plenty of stripped wood and stained glass. From outside it is difficult to believe that there are three downstairs bars, but the ample space is needed to accommodate the large crowds which frequent the place, both during the day and late into the night.

Oyster Bar `12 H7`
Market Lane
off St. Patrick Street
Phone (021) 4272716
Situated at the end of a narrow alleyway, the inside of the Oyster is rather more modern than one might imagine from looking at the 19th century shell. There are several themes on the go, from neo classical to Victorian, and there's even a bit of a bordello feel to the front portion of the bar which is furnished with comfy red velvet sofas. The overall effect is pleasing to the eye, and the bar attracts a mixed clientele during the day

and a mainly young crowd at night as the volume of the music increases. Late bar from Thursday night through to Monday night.

Pavilion `12 H7`
Carey's Lane
The Pav is a popular late night venue for the city's young clubbers.

Raven Bar `12 H7`
100 South Main Street
Phone (021) 4277307
Raven-black on the outside, and a mish-mash of modern fittings inside which struggle to make any kind of style statement, but the end result seems to be greater than the sum of its parts judging by the lively crowd which the place manages to attract.

Reardens Bar `12 G7`
26 Washington Street
Phone (021) 4271969
Cavernous bar, fitted out along traditional lines, but best known as a reliable place to get a late drink most nights of the week.

The Red Room `12 H7`
Liberty Street
Large bar cum club which attracts

The Long Valley on Winthrop Street

The Grey Hound in Kinsale

a young crowd and requires an entry fee later in the evening.

Reidy's Wine Vault `11 F7`
Western Road
Phone (021) 4275751
Lovely Victorian-style bar with black and white tiled floor, beautifully carved mahogany bar, snugs and several large upholstered booths which can accommodate large groups in comfort. All housed in a converted wine warehouse just opposite Jury's Hotel.

The Roundy `12 H7`
1 Castle Street
Phone (021) 4277682
Yes, it is round on the outside, and quite stylish within. A slate floor, painted stone walls, a bar constructed from glass and stainless steel, and a large light box feature on the far wall all combine to create a very modern but tasteful look. Coffee is as much to the fore as beer, while upstairs provides another attractive space which hosts live music, resident DJ's every Thursday and Friday, and regular theatrical productions during the summer months.

Sir Henry's `12 H7`
South Main Street
Popular late night dance club with several rooms and DJ's and an ever changing menu of club nights.

South's `12 H7`
South Mall
Part of the Imperial Hotel complex, South's is part of a new breed of superpub which does things on a grand scale. In this instance, the bar is richly fitted out on different levels with lots of dark wood and an ornate decor somewhat reminiscent of a Victorian drawing room. Business is brisk and a late bar adds to the attraction.

The Vineyard `12 H7`
Market Lane, off St. Patrick St
Phone (021) 4274793
Another top place for style gurus. Located down a narrow alleyway, it is a pleasant surprise to enter the Vineyard and find a bar which oozes sophistication. Natural daylight pours in through a skylight towards the back of the long narrow bar, the decor is subtle and understated, and the clientele tend to match their surroundings. Entertainment in the smaller upstairs bar includes a Salsa night every Thursday and Friday until late.

Yumi Yuki Club `12 H7`
Triskel Arts Centre, Tobin St
Phone (021) 4275777
Small sushi & sake bar located upstairs at the Triskel. Themed loosely along Japanese lines, the customers are suitably arty, and beer is served to those of us who have not yet developed a taste for Japanese rocket fuel. Certainly a fresh alternative to traditional Irish pubs. Look out for the special offer of film, sushi and sake, all

Decision time at Bodega - will it be black olive bread or ciabatta?

for £8 per head.

KINSALE PUBS

The 1601 `22`
Pearse Street, KINSALE
Phone (021) 4772529
Ask somebody to name a pub in Kinsale and it's a fair bet that they will mention the 1601, which is named after the date of the Battle of Kinsale. There is little to remark upon about the interior, save perhaps for the battle plan which hangs in the front bar and some dodgy art in the back bar. The pub is popular with locals and visitors alike who come to enjoy the banter and the lively atmosphere which can become quite boisterous at night time, especially when there is live music in the house.

The Dock Bar `22`
Castle Park, KINSALE
Located about a mile out of town, The Dock is a waterside bar which comes into its own whenever the sun comes out. Plenty of seating out front allows the customers to soak up a few rays, a few pints and a fabulous view.

The Grey Hound `22`
Market Square, KINSALE
Phone (021) 4772889
Set back slightly from the main drag, The Grey Hound is at its best as you enter through the front door

Mary's PR firm - otherwise known as The Tap Tavern in Kinsale

and find yourself immediately at the bar counter. This area is pleasantly time-warped, while the rest of the bar reveals itself in a slightly higgledy-piggledy fashion with very few right angles in evidence, although things do tend to straighten up after a few pints in front of the open fire.

Lord Kingsale   `22`
4 Main Street, KINSALE
Phone (021) 4772371
If you are homesick for the home counties of England, then a cure is at hand at The Lord Kingsale which feels as if it must have spent its formative years in a Surrey village. From the half-timbered walls and ceilings, to the red velvet upholstery, right down to the horse brasses on the wall, this feels like an English country pub. A bit odd

perhaps, but nonetheless a warm and comfortable refuge from the hurly burly outside.

Spaniard Inn   `22`
High Road, KINSALE
Phone (021) 4772436
Well known pub which is situated on a hairpin bend about ten minutes walk from the centre of Kinsale. Inside is reminiscent of a smugglers inn, with stone floors, an open fire, low ceilings, and a seafaring theme to the fore. The bar serves great lunches for around a fiver, and there's a separate restaurant next door. The benches out front are a good spot to grab some sunshine while you watch the world drift by, and there are a couple of outdoor tables at the back if space is at a premium. Music sessions most nights of the

week.

Tap Tavern   `22`
Guardwell, KINSALE
How appearances can deceive! At first sight, the Tap is a timeless bar which does not seem to have changed for a generation or two. The linoleum floor and simple furnishings hark back to the past, but this is not a bar to stand still. Take a look out into the new courtyard at the back of the bar and you will find an outdoor area which is heated by a real fire and a gas heater, with a retractable awning to keep the elements at bay should the need arise. Work was carried out at the end of 1999 and, in the course of demolishing some outhouses, a medieval well was discovered which dates back to the 11th century and has now been incorporated into the design. Without doubt, however, the pub's best feature is the landlady, Mary, who has spent all her life in Kinsale, probably missing out on a glittering career in the PR industry as a result. Mary is good steam and will be only too happy to keep you up to date with developments, including the bar's new web site which features her two cats, Susie and Cromwell! The spring water contract can't be too far behind.

White Lady   `22`
Lower O'Connell Street
KINSALE
Phone (021) 4772737
Once you have completed your pub crawl of Kinsale and are feeling ready to strut your stuff on the dance floor, the White Lady is probably the best nightclub the town has to offer. If you don't fancy the five minute walk or the length of the queue, a more convenient alternative is **Bacchus Niteclub** at **Kieran's Folk House Inn** on Guardwell.

There are hundreds of restaurants and cafés to choose from in Cork and Kinsale but this guide attempts to select about 35 of the best. This process is bound to be subjective but no apologies are made for that. After all, how many times have you eaten at a restaurant for the first time because it happened to be recommended to you by somebody else?

All establishments featured have been tried out, often frequently, by somebody connected with the Cork & Kinsale Guide. They have been selected by people who enjoy good food and drink, bearing in mind price, location and diversity. These places are the ones that we have enjoyed most - the ones that we recommend to friends and relatives. They don't always agree, and perhaps you won't either, but that's what being subjective is all about! Having said that, we would be keen to hear your own recommendations or any objections that you might have regarding any of our choices.

What can be said, without fear of contradiction, is that the restaurant scene in county Cork has been transformed over the past ten years. Choice and quality have improved tremendously, and this trend looks set to continue. Kinsale has earned the tag of 'gourmet capital of Ireland' due to the proliferation of small owner-run establishments, offering an exciting choice of menus and a level of culinary excellence which has been stimulated by stiff competition. The highpoint of the gastronomic year is the **Kinsale Gourmet Festival** which is organised by the town's Good Food Circle, usually around mid-October. Kinsale does not have a monopoly on good food, however, and Cork City has many excellent restaurants which can hold their own against most of their European counterparts.

Many are mentioned in the growing array of good food guides.

Price Rating

£	Cheap (usually under £12 per head)
££	Moderate (between £12 and £25)
£££	Expensive (£25+)

These publications all have their good points but, invariably, one area of contention is their attempts to estimate the likely cost of a meal. We have all had the experience of going somewhere supposedly "cheap & cheerful" only to find that a couple of drinks and a shared bottle of wine can do strange things to the bill. On the other hand, there are occasions when you may have taken advantage of a very reasonable fixed price menu, and left with both your conscience and the contents of your wallet largely intact!

When you add in lunchtime and early evening specials, fixed-price menus, and happy hours, attempts to estimate price often tend to be in vain. The system adopted for this guide, therefore, is rather broad-brush in its approach, attempting to categorise a restaurant as expensive, moderate or cheap.

"Expensive" restaurants are those where you can expect the final bill to exceed £25 per head. If you eat somewhere categorised as "cheap", you will, more often than not, escape for under a tenner. The final bill at a restaurant falling into the moderate category should fall somewhere between £12 and £25, bearing in mind all the caveats mentioned earlier.

Finally, the golden rule when using this guide is to phone first! All the information included was gathered in spring 2000, but restaurants come and go, change ownership, chefs, menus, opening hours and much else, so it is best to check with the restaurant before turning up to eat.

Arbutus Lodge `13` `L5`
Montenotte, Cork
Phone (021) 450 1237
Price Rating: £££
The Arbutus Lodge is a family run hotel and restaurant housed in an elegant Georgian residence which was once home to the Lord Mayor of Cork. The food lives up to the grand surroundings and is complemented by an award winning wine list which is among the most comprehensive to be found anywhere in Ireland. Lunch in the Gallery Bar is a more casual alternative to the formality of the dining room.

Ballymaloe House
Shanagarry
Nr Midleton, Co Cork
Phone (021) 4652531
Price Rating: £££
Situated on a 400 acre estate, about half an hour's drive from the centre of Cork, this legend in Irish culinary circles will not disappoint. If proof were needed that it is possible to push the boat out occasionally and yet get fantastic value for your money, this is it. The Ballymaloe experience begins with its attractive

Kinsale Gourmet Store

Cafe Paradiso vegetarian restaurant on Lancaster Quay

rural setting and the Georgian grandeur of the house, the stylish comfort of the drawing room where you can enjoy an aperitif while perusing the menu, the attentive service and, of course, the fabulous food, most of which is sourced locally. The fixed price lunch menu comes in at around £20 per head while dinner will cost around £35. Remember to fast long and hard before you arrive. *Opening Times: Mon-Sun 1pm-2pm & 7pm-9.30pm*

Bewley's `12 H7`
Cook Street, Cork
Price Rating: £
Bewley's Oriental Cafes are famous throughout Ireland, but the magic of the Grafton Street flagship in Dublin has never really been repli-

cated. Having said that, the Cork outlet is a popular spot to fortify yourself with the all day traditional Irish breakfast, or to rest your weary feet while enjoying your favourite blend of freshly brewed tea or coffee and nibbling on something from the mouthwatering selection of home-baked pastries.

Bully's `12 H7`
40 Paul Street, Cork
Phone (021) 4273555
Price Rating: £
Small, cheap and cheerful restaurant offering a good choice of burgers, pizzas, pasta and plenty more besides, including a few veggy options. Other branches in Douglas and Bishopstown areas of the city. *Opening Times: Mon-Sat 12noon-*

11.30pm; Sun 1pm-11.30pm

Cafe Mexicana `12 H7`
Carey's Lane, Cork
Phone (021) 4276433
Traditional Mexican cantina situated just off Patrick's Street. Menu includes the usual suspects - tacos, burritos, enchiladas and fajitas. *Open daily 12noon until late.*

Cafe Paradiso `12 G7`
16 Lancaster Quay, Cork
Phone (021) 4277939
Price Rating: ££
You don't have to be vegetarian to enjoy what's on offer at Cafe Paradiso. Doors open in the morning for coffee and snacks but lunch and dinner present a better opportunity to sample vegetarian cooking which is carried out with considerable style and imagination, reflecting influences from far beyond Irish shores. Its growing reputation means that things are usually buzzing but, if you can't get a table, you can always retreat to your own kitchen with a copy of the Cafe Paradiso Cookbook! *Opening Times: Tues-Sat 10.30am-10.30pm*

China Garden `12 H7`
French Church Street, Cork
Phone (021) 4276455
Price Rating: ££
Popular Chinese restaurant offering a wide selection of delicious oriental cuisine. The 4 course high tea, served 5.30pm-7pm Monday to Friday, is especially good value at £7.50 per head. *Opening Times: Mon-Sat 12.30pm-2.30pm & 5.30pm-12.30am; Sun 5pm-12midnight*

Coal Quay Cafe `12 H7`
Cornmarket St, Cork
Phone (021) 4272880
Price Rating: ££
Along with Bodega next door, Coal Quay is doing its bit to bring a bit of modern style to Cork's eating and drinking circle. White-washed

stone walls, a beech floor, potted palms and lots of natural light pouring in through skylights all help to promote a light and airy feel. The menu is broad-ranging but focussed, so that even the most indecisive should find it relatively simple to choose from a selection which includes duck, chicken, lamb and fish, all beautifully prepared and presented. *Opening Times: Wed-Sun 5.30pm until late*

Crawford Gallery Cafe `12 H6`
Emmet Place, Cork
Phone (021) 4274415
Price Rating: £
Situated in Cork's leading art gallery, the cafe is managed by Fern Allen, daughter of Myrtle Allen of Ballymaloe fame, and this connection helps to ensure that seats are at a premium all day long. Whether it's breakfast, lunch or afternoon tea, the food and the service live up to the family reputation. There's a choice of about half a dozen main courses at lunchtime, all for under a tenner and, if you don't want to miss out on the delicious desserts, the three course lunch for £13 offers an attractive option. Finally, whether you need to or not, pop upstairs and appreciate the architectural wonder of what must be the hippest loos in Cork. *Opening Times: Mon-Sat 10am-5pm*

Esau's `12 H7`
Carey's Lane
Price Rating: £
Cool and modern restaurant serving mainly Italian style food at reasonable prices. *Opening Times: 12.30pm-4pm & 6pm-10pm*

Farmgate Cafe `12 H7`
English Market
Princes Street, Cork
Phone (021) 4278134
Price Rating: £
Even for those of us who don't believe in the benefits of retail therapy, a wander round Cork's English Market, a giant Victorian food hall, is always a colourful and enjoyable experience. Farmgate Cafe looks down from a balcony position onto the anthill below, providing an ideal spot to watch life go by while enjoying the farm-fresh produce which is the hallmark of the cafe. *Opening Times: Mon-Sat 8.30am-5pm*

Gambieni's Restaurant `12 H7`
Carey's Lane
Phone (021) 4272388
Price Rating: £
Italian restaurant offering a good choice of main courses including plenty of inexpensive pizzas and pasta options, all served up in slightly rustic surroundings. *Open 12noon-12midnight*

Gingerbread House `12 H7`
Paul Street, Cork
Price Rating: £
One of the busiest eateries in town where you can eat your fill without putting much of a dent in your budget. Hansel & Grethal may have inspired the name, but the look and feel is that of a large Irish country kitchen, perhaps with the exception of the cuckoo clock! A mega Irish breakfast is available until noon and will set you back only £3. Soup, sandwiches and a great selection of

The Coal Quay on Cornmarket St

breads, cakes and pastries are on offer, and a take away service is available during the hectic lunchtime period. The current menu will be bolstere by the addition of a pizza and crepes bar which is about to open at the time of writing.

Gino's `12 H7`
7 Winthrop Street, Cork
Phone (021) 4274485
Price Rating: £
Popular Italian ice cream joint which serves very good pizzas into the bargain.

Isaacs Restaurant `12 J6`
48 MacCurtain Street, Cork
Phone (021) 4503805
Price Rating: ££
Why can't all restaurants be like

Spring breaking out at Ballymaloe

Isaacs Restaurant on MacCurtain St

this? The impressive dining room has the feel of a light and spacious wine vault with a tiled floor and painted brick walls and arches which are warmed by a collection of modern art. The service is attentive, but friendly, and the interesting bistro-style menu delivers food which invariably tastes superb. And the fact that you can have all this and still have lunch for a tenner means that there's always an enjoyable hustle and bustle about the place. *Opening Times: Mon-Sat 10am-10.30pm; Sun 6pm-9.30pm*

Ivory Tower `12 H7`
35 Princes Street, Cork
Phone (021) 4274665
Price Rating: £££
The unprepossessing frontage may not look overly inspiring but, behind the facade, culinary excitement awaits in the upstairs dining room. The Ivory Tower is rightly renowned for the cutting edge nature of the cooking, with inspiration being drawn from around the globe. *Opening Times: Wed-Sun 6pm-11pm*

Jacobs on the Mall `12 H7`
30A South Mall, Cork
Phone (021) 4251530
Price Rating: £££
It might look like a bank or an office building from the outside but Jacob's used to be a Turkish bath house in a former life. The combination of top class, modern European cuisine and the elegance of the dining room make Jacob's one of the best restaurants in town. *Opening Times: Mon-Sat 12.30pm-2.30pm & 6.30pm-10pm*

Jacques `12 J7`
Phoenix Street, Cork
Phone (021) 4277387
Price Rating: £££
Long established restaurant where both the cooking and the decor are creative and adventurous. It doesn't come cheap but your palate is unlikely to regret the food, although you might not agree where the colour scheme is concerned. The two course early dinner menu offers terrific value at £12 a head and is available between 6pm and 7pm. *Opening Times: Mon-Fri 12noon-3pm & 6pm-10.30pm; Sat 6pm-10pm*

Meadows & Byrne `12 H7`
Academy Street, Cork
Bustling cafe situated at the back of one of Cork's leading outlets for houseware. Grab one of the few tables and ponder a potential purchase over a cup of excellent coffee or fortify yourself with breakfast, which is served from 8.30, or a bite of lunch. A few tables outside, weather permitting.

Jacobs on South Mall

Milano `12 H7`
Oliver Plunkett St, Cork
Price Rating: £
Behind the mock Grecian facade lies a light, spacious, open-plan restaurant which displays all the familiar hallmarks of the British chain, Pizza Express, who operate in Ireland under the name, Milano. Expect friendly service and, arguably, the best pizzas in town, although alternatives are limited to a couple of pasta dishes and a couple of salads. This simple but winning formula means that things can be very busy but it's usually worth the wait. A no-booking policy is the norm except for large groups.

Milano on Oliver Plunkett Street

New Indian Palace `12 H7`
31 Princes Street, Cork
Phone 4273690 Price Rating: ££
Indian restaurant serving a broad selection of dishes which include plenty of vegetarian options in addition to some excellent tandoori, balti, and curry dishes.

No 5 Fenns Quay `12 G7`
Sheares Street, Cork
Phone (021) 4279527
Price Rating: ££
Fenns Quay does not overlook the river as one might expect, but the tastefully designed interior of this Georgian terrace more than makes up for the lack of a view. The modern bistro food, like the decor, is simple but stylish with a list of daily specials to complement the dinner menu. Open from 10am for coffee and snacks, but worth making a lunch or dinner date to enjoy the full experience of one of the best restaurants in Cork. *Opening Times: Mon-Sat 10am-10pm*

Proby's Bistro `12 H7`
Proby's Quay, Cork
Phone (021) 4316531
Price Rating: ££
Situated close to St Fin Barre's Cathedral, Proby's is a modern restaurant offering bistro food and a piano bar which helps to cultivate a warm and friendly atmosphere. *Open for lunch & dinner Mon-Sat*

Quay Co-op `12 H7`
24 Sullivan Quay
Phone (021) 4317660
Price Rating: £
Located above an impressive health food store, the Quay Co-op has been catering to Cork's vegetarians for many years. At first sight the menu might not appear to be particularly veggy, with burgers, pizza and lasagne all on offer in addition to the list of daily specials, but meat is nowhere to be found. Whether you opt for a full meal or settle for a healthy snack, the emphasis is on

The Vintage Restaurant in Kinsale

wholesome food and good value. *Opening Times: Mon-Sat 9am-9pm*

Ristorante Rossini `12 H7`
33 Princes Street, Cork
Phone (021) 4275818
Price Rating: ££
Don't be put off by the slightly dodgy frontage - this is a busy Italian restaurant for good reason. The extensive menu offers a great choice of pizzas and pasta as well as some tasty meat and fish options. *Open Mon-Sun*

Ruen Thai `12 H7`
71-72 St Patrick's Street
Price Rating: ££
Phone (021) 4276127
Situated above Boots the chemist, Ruen Thai is justifiably proud of its authenticity. Thai-owned, the staff wear national dress, the restaurant is decorated in traditional style and,

most importantly, the food is prepared by a group of chefs brought over from Thailand to produce food which tends to be hot and spicy, yet easy on the palate. The menu includes plenty of meat, fish and vegetarian options.

Scoozi `12 H7`
Winthrop Lane, Cork
Phone (021) 4275077
Price Rating: £
Tucked away a little bit, this surprisingly large restaurant is decked out in country kitchen fashion, with lots of pine and plenty of curios and artefacts on show. There's usually a buzz about the place, and a fun atmosphere is promoted by a legion of young waiting staff who aren't shy when it comes to engaging in a bit of banter. The extensive menu concentrates on a selection of hamburgers, pizzas, pastas, steaks and

Max's Wine Bar & Restaurant in Kinsale

salads. Breakfast is served between 9am and 12noon. The prices offer great value and a kiddies menu is served all day. *Open daily 9am-11pm (until 10pm Sun)*

Valpariso `12 H7`
115 Oliver Plunkett St, Cork
Phone (021) 4275488
Price Rating: ££
Lots of stripped wood and sunny colours dominate the decor in an attempt to conjure up a mediterranean ambience. The cuisine is Spanish with a good selection of tapas on offer if you decide not to opt for a main course. *Opening Times: 5pm-11pm*

Yumi Yuki `12 H7`
Tobin Street, Cork
Phone (021) 4275777
Price Rating: ££
Housed upstairs in the Triskel Arts Centre, Yumi Yuki is a fun kind of place. You can eat in the small sushi & sake bar or in the slightly larger restaurant on the same floor. The Japanese theme has been completed on a limited budget, so don't expect a replica of London's Yo Sushi, although the look is suitably minimalist and the sushi comes on colour coded plates which indicate the price. Food is served 12noon-12midnight.

KINSALE RESTAURANTS

Janey Macs `22`
Main St, KINSALE
Phone (021) 4773179
Price Rating: ££
Cosy seafood restaurant and wine bar where the fish is always fresh and delicious and the emphasis is on locally sourced ingredients. Meat eaters and vegetarians are also catered for.

Kinsale Gourmet Store `22`
& Seafood Bar
KINSALE
Situated just off Market Square, the Gourmet Store adopts a refreshingly modern approach with its deli-style set up which includes a few tables inside and a few more outside, weather permitting. The seafood hits your plate within hours of leaving the water and a great lunch is on offer for under a tenner. Closes at 6pm

Man Friday's `22`
Scilly, KINSALE
Phone (021) 4772260
Price Rating: £££
Situated on high ground overlooking Kinsale Harbour, Man Friday's is a long established stalwart at the centre of Kinsale's Good Food Circle. The restaurant occupies several rooms and a garden terrace which looks like it might have been constructed by Robinson Crusoe himself. The menu is broad ranging with plenty of seafood, meat and vegetarian options. *Opening Times: Mon-Sat 7pm-10.30pm*

Max's Wine Bar `22`
Main Street, KINSALE
Phone (021) 4772443
Price Rating: ££
Attractive little restaurant offering a good choice of fish, meat, poultry and vegetarian options. The food is beautifully cooked and offers great value, especially the 3 course early bird menu for £12.50 which is available until 7.30pm. Lunch for less than £10. *Open: Mon-Sun 12.30pm-3pm & 6.30pm-10.30pm*

The Vintage Restaurant `22`
50 Main St, KINSALE
Phone (021) 4772502
Price Rating: £££
'Cosy & distinctive' is how they describe themselves and that's a pretty fair assessment given the low ceilings, the old beams and the open fires. The menu is dominated by fish and game, the cooking is straightforward and classical, and the service is professional and unobtrusive. Dinner from 6.30pm